Franklin As A Chess Player

VOL. XIV. No. 16

PRICE 10 CEN

OLD PENN

WEEKLY REVIEW
OF THE
VNIVERSITY OF PENNSYLVANI

FOVNDED ·

· IN 1740 ·

ANDRE KOROMAN

CLASS

PHILADELPHIA, PA., JANUARY 15, 1916.

UNIVERSITY OF PENNSYLVANIA
Founded by Benjamin Franklin

Provost, EDGAR F. SMITH, LL.D.   Vice-Provost, JOSIAH H. PENNIMAN, LL.D.

THE COLLEGE. *Dean*, ARTHUR H. QUINN, Ph.D.—This School comprises the following courses, all of which are open to men and women excepting Arts and Science.

ARTS AND SCIENCE.—Four years; A.B. Tuition, $150.

Students in the Arts and Science course may combine their course with that of Medicine so that both may be finished in seven years. In a similar way with Architecture, in six years.

MUSIC.—Four years, leading to a certificate of proficiency, and after one year to the degree of B.M. Tuition $30.

BIOLOGY.—Four years; B.S. in Biology. Two years' special course preparatory to Medicine; also another two years' special course in Biology, embracing Botany, Zoology and Anatomy, and leading to a certificate of proficiency. Tuition $150.

COLLEGE COURSES FOR TEACHERS.—Courses similar to those in Arts and Science leading to degree upon completion of required number of units. Tuition, $10 per year for each hour of instruction.

SUMMER SCHOOL.—Sessions daily for six weeks, beginning the second week of July. Courses in most College subjects. Tuition, $15 for the first lecture course, and $10 for each additional course. Laboratory courses, $20 to $30.

WHARTON SCHOOL OF FINANCE AND COMMERCE. *Dean*, R. C. McCREA, Ph.D.—Four years. For men entering a business career, public service, law, or social work. B.S. in Economics. Tuition, $150.

EVENING SCHOOL OF ACCOUNTS AND FINANCE in Philadelphia: *Secretary*, GEORGE A. MacFARLANE, B.S.—Three years of University work, leading to a certificate. Tuition, $70.

EXTENSION SCHOOLS OF ACCOUNTS AND FINANCE in Scranton, Wilkesbarre, Harrisburg and Reading, PA.; *Secretary*, GEORGE A. MacFARLANE, B.S.—Three years of University work, leading to a certificate. Tuition, $50.

THE TOWNE SCIENTIFIC SCHOOL. *Dean*, JOHN FRAZER, Ph.D.—Which includes the following courses:

ARCHITECTURE.—Four years; B.S. in Architecture. Also special two-year course for qualified architectural draftsmen; also one graduate year, leading to master's degree. Tuition, $200.

ELECTRICAL ENGINEERING.—Four years; B.S. in Electrical Engineering. Tuition, $200.

MECHANICAL ENGINEERING.—Four years; B.S. in Mechanical Engineering. Tuition, $200.

CIVIL ENGINEERING.—Four years; B.S. in Civil Engineering. Tuition, $200.

CHEMISTRY AND CHEMICAL ENGINEERING.—Four years; B.S. in Chemistry or B.S. in Chemical Engineering. Tuition, $200.

GRADUATE SCHOOL. *Dean*, HERMAN V. AMES, Ph.D.—Offers advanced instruction in the various branches of Literature and Science, leading to the degrees of M.A. and Ph.D.

Twenty-six fellowships, for men, awarded annually; free tuition, and a stipend of from $500 to $800.

Six fellowships, for women, granting free tuition and stipend of $200 and $225.

Eight scholarships, for men, granting free tuition and $100.

Also thirty University fellowships and scholarships covering tuition fees.

Tuition, $12.50 per standard course of one hour a week throughout the year. Maximum, $150 per year.

LAW SCHOOL. *Dean*, WILLIAM E. MIKELL, LL.M.—Course of three years, leading to the degree of LL.B. The courses are so conducted that the student may acquire not only a knowledge of the rules of law, but also the ability to deal with legal problems. The "Case System" of instruction is used. Course fits students for practice in any State. Besides the regular curriculum, the student has an opportunity to attend a number of courses on special subjects given by the members of the auxiliary teaching force. Graduates may become candidates for the degree of LL.M. Tuition, $200.

MEDICINE. *Dean*, WILLIAM PEPPER, M.D.—Course of four years divided into two periods of two years each, the first period devoted to the fundamental medical sciences, Anatomy, Physiological Chemistry, Physiology. Pharmacology and Pathology; the second period to the clinical subjects, Medicine, Surgery, Obstetrics and the specialties. The degree of M.D. is conferred upon all graduates. The teaching staff numbers 173. The facilities for instruction both in the laboratory and clinical subjects are unexcelled in point of equipment. Tuition, $200.

COURSES IN PUBLIC HEALTH, open to graduates of Medicine, extending over one academic session and leading to degree of D.P.H. (Doctor of Public Hygiene). Tuition, $150.

COURSES IN TROPICAL MEDICINE.—Open to graduates in Medicine; extend from opening of session to about February 1; lead to certificate. Tuition, $150.

HOSPITAL FACILITIES.—The University Hospital, in which there are fourteen wards, with a total capacity of 400 beds; the University has special privileges for instruction at the Philadelphia General Hospital, which adjoins the University, and in which there are more than five thousand patients.

STUDENTS' WARD.—A special ward is maintained for the care of students, only a slight charge being made for board.

TRAINING SCHOOL FOR NURSES.—The course of instruction covers a period of three years.

WILLIAM PEPPER CLINICAL LABORATORY.—Devoted to graduate work for the prosecution of minute studies in original researches.

WISTAR INSTITUTE.—Devoted to research work on Anatomy, and containing the Wistar and Horner Museums of Biology and Anatomy. Publishes five scientific journals.

LABORATORY OF HYGIENE.—Devoted to special research work in Hygiene and Bacteriology.

THE PHIPPS INSTITUTE.—For the Study, Prevention and Treatment of Tuberculosis. Offers exceptional opportunity for observation along special lines.

LABORATORY OF RESEARCH MEDICINE.—Devoted to research in Medicine.

DENTISTRY. *Dean*, EDWARD C. KIRK, D.D.S., Sc.D.—Course of three years; beginning with fall of 1917, course will be four years. The laboratory method of instruction forms an important part of the training, not only in the practical dental branches, but in the elementary scientific subjects of Chemistry, Anatomy, Physiology, and Bacteriology, etc. The school is housed in the Evans Dental Institute Building. The degree of D.D.S. is conferred upon graduates. Tuition, $200.

A POST-GRADUATE COURSE IN DENTISTRY, extending over one year, is open to graduates in Dentistry.

VETERINARY MEDICINE. *Dean*, LOUIS A. KLEIN, V.M.D.—Four years, and leading to the degree of V.M.D.; qualifies graduates for general practice, for Federal, State and Municipal inspection of meat and milk, and for investigation of Veterinary problems and for teaching. Tuition, $100.

THE SCHOOL OF EDUCATION. *Dean*, FRANK P. GRAVES, LL.D.—Four years leading to degree of B.S. in Education. Tuition, $160.

Administrative Officers

EDWARD ROBINS, A.M., *Secretary*   WILLIAM H. HUTT, JR., *Treasurer*   GEORGE E. NITZSCHE, LL.B., *Recorder*
WILLIAM O. MILLER, A.B., *Bursar*

GENERAL UNIVERSITY ADVANTAGES

UNIVERSITY LIBRARY.—The collection contains more than 400,000 volumes and 50,000 pamphlets. It includes many special libraries, as well as a number of departmental libraries. The Biddle Law Library contains almost 70,000 volumes.

PHYSICAL EDUCATION.—The Gymnasium comprises Weightman Hall, three smaller exercising rooms, and a large swimming pool, with locker rooms and shower bath. It overlooks FRANKLIN FIELD, used for track and field sports. Provision is made for medical and physical examination of all students by the Director, and for the prescription of exercise in suitable cases.

Among the places of general interest are: THE UNIVERSITY MUSEUM OF ARCHAEOLOGY, which contains valuable Babylonian, Etruscan, Egyptian and Mediterranean collections, and one of the most complete American and general ethnological collections; the FLOWER ASTRONOMICAL OBSERVATORY, on the West Chester Pike, which is fully equipped with modern telescopes and instruments; and the BOTANIC GARDENS AND GREENHOUSES. These are all open to the public.

RELIGIOUS ACTIVITIES.—Under the auspices of the Christian Association of the University. Services by eminent ministers are conducted each Sunday morning in Houston Hall, also daily voluntary Chapel exercises.

THE DORMITORIES consist of twenty-nine houses, inclosing three beautiful courtyards. The average price paid by students for board and lodging is $5.50 per week.

THE HOUSTON CLUB.—The Houston Club is the exponent of the social side of Pennsylvania student life. Its home is Houston Hall.

CAMPUS AND EQUIPMENT.—The campus of the University covers more than a hundred acres and is about ten minutes from City Hall, the center of a population of a million and a half. The equipment consists of about seventy buildings.

For General Information Address **University Recorder.**

For Special Information Address **Heads of Departments.**

A DORMITORY ARCHWAY.

OLD PENN

WEEKLY REVIEW OF THE UNIVERSITY OF PENNSYLVANIA

FRANKLIN AS A CHESS PLAYER.

His Famous Essay on the Morals of Chess.

Chess may not be a road to greatness, but it is nevertheless true that most great men have followed the road for diversion and found in it certain virtuous elements which are very admirably set forth in the first essay on the game published in America.

The illustration shows the members of the "Good Companion Problem Club" composed partly of Franklin Club members gathered around America's most historic and interesting set of chess men, the original set owned by Benjamin Franklin. Most of

SOME MEMBERS OF THE FRANKLIN CHESS CLUB.

entitled "The Morals of Chess," by Benjamin Franklin and contributed to "The Columbian Magazine" of December 1786, for the privilege of reference to which we are indebted to Mr. James F. Magee, Jr., '87 C., a member of the Franklin Chess Club.

Before considering "The Morals of Chess" it may be interesting to note that Philadelphia has always played an important part in the chess world and has several noted chess clubs among which the Franklin Chess Club is the most prominent.

our alumni of chess circles will recognize standing in background at the left, G. W. McAllister, S. W. Bampton and Rev. B. M. Neill, formerly of Asbury Church and a frequent player at the University. Russell Duane, '91 L., standing on the left is the owner of the Franklin men and J. F. Magee, Jr., '87 C., is standing in front of Mr. Bampton.

Franklin's chess men are made from box and rose wood, they are not show pieces as they have seen hard usage. For over fifty-five years the Patriot

517

sought recreation in playing the Royal game; from 1734 until his death he many times mentioned the game in his autobiography.

The chess men are of French workmanship, as the French fou or fool decorated on the top with the three-cornered hat of the Jacobin or court jester, designates.

It is remarkable that we are able to include in this sketch two pictures of Franklin playing chess, both from old numbers of "Harper's," one representing the first game of American chess, to which we can affix a date, 1734, between Franklin and an un-

BENJAMIN FRANKLIN'S CHESS MEN.

named friend in Philadelphia, and the other between Franklin and Lady Howe, in London, in 1774.

In his autobiography, Franklin says:

"I had begun in 1733 to study languages (he was then 27 years old); I soon made myself so much a master of the French, as to be able to read the books in that language with ease. I then undertook the Italian. An acquaintance who was also learning it, used often to tempt me to play chess with him. (It is curious that chess players ever since, have claimed that they are tempted by others to play.) Finding this took up too much of the time I had to spare for study, I at length refused to play any more unless on this condition, that the victor in every game should have the right to impose a task, either of parts of grammar to be got by heart, or in translations, which tasks the vanquished was to perform, upon honor, before our next meeting. As we played pretty equally, we thus beat one another into that language."

That he frequently yielded to similar temptations is indicated by the following additional extracts from his autobiography:

"Honest David Martin, Rector of our Academy, my principal antagonist at chess is dead, and a few remaining players here are indifferent, so that I have no need of Stamma's 12 sh. pamphlet, and am glad you did not send it." (Philadelphia, 1752.)*

My dear child (His wife, Deborah): "Please send me the Indian Sealskin Hussiff, with all the things that were in it . . . Among my books on the shelves there are two or three little pieces on the game of chess. One in French, bound in leather 8 vo., one in a blue paper cover, English; two others in manuscript, one of them thin in brown paper cover, the other in loose leaves, not bound. If you can find them yourself, send them; but do not send anybody else to look for them. You may know the French one by the word 'Echecs' on the title page." (New York, 1757.)

"Mrs. French understands that Doctor Franklin dines with the Bishop of St. Asaph's to-morrow, hopes he will do her ye favor of dining with her on Wednesday or Thursday, both days will be giving her a double pleasure; she has provided chess players for each day." (England, June, 1775.)

"You know Md. Brillon's gardens, and what fine walks they contain. . . . During the summer you went there at six o'clock. You found the charming lady, with her lovely children and friends, eager to walk with you and entertain you with their agreeable conversation; and what has been your choice? Why, to sit on the terrace, satisfying yourself with fine prospects, and passing your eyes over the beauties of the garden below, without taking one step to descend and walk about them. On the contrary, you call for tea, and the chess board; and lo! you are occupied in your seat till nine o'clock, and that besides two hours play after dinner." (Paris, written at midnight, October 22, 1780.)

Count von Bruhl's letter to Dr. Franklin, London, 1783. "Sir:—I was very much flattered with the letter I had the pleasure to receive from your excellency by means of the ingenious M-de Kempel's arrival in England. The favorable opinion you entertain of his talents is alone sufficient to convince me of their extent and usefulness. I cannot find words to express the gratitude I feel for the honour of your remembrance." This letter is evidently a reply to Franklin's communication, urging Von Bruhl to be sure and visit the chess automaton (invented in Vienna, 1769, burnt in Philadelphia, 1854) upon its arrival in London.

Franklin's "Morals of Chess" was reprinted by James Humphreys, 1766 College, in one of those little three-by-four, vellum or leather-covered volumes, so familiar and dear to the bibliophile. He was a bookseller and editor of the "Pennsylvania Gazette," a Tory newspaper. It was also translated into French and Russian, and so after a somewhat tedious preamble we come to the Essay itself:

TO THE EDITOR OF THE COLUMBIAN MAGAZINE:

Sir—Playing at chess is the most ancient and most universal game known among men; for its origin is beyond the memory of history, and it has for numberless ages, been the amusement of all the

---

*David Martin was the first Rector of the Academy, 1749-51, and Professor of Greek and Latin.

civilized nations of Asia, the Persians, the Indians, and the Chinese, Europe has had it above 1,000 years; the Spaniards have spread it over their part of America, and it begins lately to make its appearance in these northern States. It is so interesting in itself, as not to need the view of gain to induce engaging in it; and hence it is never played for money.

FRANKLIN AND FRIEND PLAYING CHESS,
PHILADELPHIA, 1734.

Those therefore who have leisure for such diversions, cannot find one that is more innocent; and the following piece, written with a view to correct (among a few young friends) some little improprieties in the practice of it, shows at the same time, that it may in its effects on the mind, be not merely innocent, but advantageous, to the vanquished as well as the victor.

THE MORALS OF CHESS.

The game of chess is not merely an idle amusement. Several very valuable qualities of the mind, useful in the course of human life, are to be acquired or strengthened by it, so as to become habits, ready on all occasions. For life is a kind of chess, in which we have often points to gain, and competitors or adversaries to contend with, and in which there is a vast variety of good and ill events, that are, in some degree, the effects of prudence or the want of it. By playing at chess, then, we may learn:

1. Foresight, which looks a little into futurity, and considers the consequences that may attend an action; for it is continually occurring to the player. "If I move this piece, what will be the advantages of my new situation? What use can my adversary make of it to annoy me? What other moves can I make to support it, and to defend myself from his attacks?"

2. Circumspection, which surveys the whole chess board, or scene of action, the relations of the several pieces and situations, the dangers they are respectively exposed to, the several probabilities that their aiding each other; the probabilities that the adversary may make this or that move, and attack this or the other piece; and what different means can be used to avoid his stroke, or turn its consequences against him.

3. Caution, not to make our moves too hastily. This habit is best acquired by observing strictly the laws of the game, such as: If you touch a piece you must move it somewhere; if you let it down, you must let it stand. And it is therefore best that these rules should be observed, as the game thereby becomes more the image of human life, and particularly of war; in which, if you have incautiously put yourself into a bad and dangerous position, you cannot obtain your enemy's leave to withdraw your troops, and place them more securely; but you must abide all the consequences of your rashness. And lastly we learn by chess the habit of not being discouraged by present bad appearances in the state of our affairs, the habit of hoping for a favorable change, and that of persevering in the search of resources. The game is so full of events, there is such a variety of turns in it, the fortune of it is so subject to sudden vicissitudes, and one so frequently, after long contemplation, discovers the means of extricating one's self from a supposed insurmountable difficulty, that one is encouraged to continue the contest to the last, in hopes that victory by our own skill, or, at least of giving a stale mate by the negligence of our adversary. And whoever considers what in chess he often sees instances of, that particular pieces of success are apt to produce presumption, and its consequent, inattention, by which more is afterwards lost than was gained by the preceding advantage; while misfortunes produce more care and attention, by which the loss may be recovered, will learn not to be too much discouraged by the present success of his adversary, nor to despair of final good fortune, upon every little check he receives in pursuit of it.

That we may therefore be induced more frequently

FRANKLIN AND LADY HOWE PLAYING CHESS,
LONDON, 1774.

to choose this beneficial amusement, in preference to others which are not attended with the same advantages, every circumstance that may increase the pleasure of it should be regarded; and every action or word that is unfair, disrespectful, or that in any way may give uneasiness, should be avoided, as contrary to the immediate intention of both the players, which is to pass their time agreeably. Therefore:

1. If it is agreed to play according to the strict rules, then those rules are to be exactly observed by both parties; and should not be insisted on for one side, while deviated from by the other, for this is not equitable.

2. If it is agreed not to observe the rules exactly,

but one party demands indulgences, he should then be as willing to allow them to the other.

3. No false move should ever be made to extricate yourself out of a difficulty, or to gain an advantage.

LA MORALE

DES

ÉCHECS.

Traduit de l'Anglois ,

DE B. FRANKLIN.

P A R I S ,

1 7 9 2.

TITLE PAGE OF THE FRENCH TRANSLATION.

There can be no pleasure in playing with a person once detected in such unfair practice.

4. If your adversary is long in playing, you ought not to hurry him, or express any uneasiness at his delay. You should not sing, nor whistle, nor look at your watch, nor take up a book to read, nor make a tapping with your feet on the floor, or with your fingers on the table, nor do anything that may disturb his attention. For all these things displease. And they do not show your skill in playing, but your craftiness, or your rudeness.

5. You ought not to endeavor to amuse and deceive your adversary by pretending to have made bad moves, and saying you have now lost the game, in order to make him secure and careless, and inattentive to your schemes; for this is fraud and deceit, not skill in the game.

6. You must not, when you have gained a victory,

520

use any triumphing or insulting expression, nor show too much pleasure, but endeavor to console your adversary, and make him less dissatisfied with himself by every kind and civil expression, that may be used with truth; such as, you understand the game better than I, but you are a little inattentive; or, you play too fast; or, you had the best of the game, but something happened to divert your thoughts, and that turned it in my favor.*

CHESS MADE EASY.

NEW AND COMPREHENSIVE

RULES

FOR PLAYING THE

GAME OF CHESS;

WITH EXAMPLES FROM

PHILIDOR, CUNNINGHAM,

&c. &c.

To which is prefixed

A pleasing account of its Origin ; some interesting anecdotes of several exalted Personages who have been admirers of it; and the

Morals of Chess,

Written by the ingenious and learned

DR. FRANKLIN.

This Game an Indian Brahmin did invent,
The force of Eastern wisdom to express;
From thence the same to busy Europe sent,
The modern Lombards stil'd it pensive Chess.
DENHAM.

Philadelphia:

PRINTED AND SOLD BY JAMES HUMPHREYS,
At the Corner of Walnut and Dock-ftreets.
....
1802.

TITLE PAGE OF HUMPHREY'S REPRINT.

7. If you are a spectator, while others play, observe the most perfect silence. For, if you give advice, you offend both parties, him against whom you gave it, because it may cause the loss of his game; him in whose favor you gave it, because though it

*If Franklin followed these rules consistently, every true lover of chess will concede him to have been the very king of chess players, a knight without fear and without reproach.

ПРАВИЛА

для

ШАШЕЧНОЙ

ИГРЫ

СОЧИНЕННЫЯ ФРАНКЛИНОМЪ,

и

Переведенныя

съ

Французскаго языка.

Печатано

ВЪ САНКТПЕТЕРБУРГѢ
1791 года.

TITLE PAGE OF THE RUSSIAN TRANSLATION.

may be good, and he follows it, he loses the pleasure
he might have had, if you had permitted him to think
until it had occurred to himself. Even after a move
or moves, you must not, by replacing the pieces, show
how it might have been played better; for that dis-
pleases and may occasion disputes or doubts about
their true situation. All talking to the players les-
sens or diverts their attention and is therefore un-
pleasing; nor should you give the least hint to either
party, by any kind of noise or motion. If you do, you
are unworthy to be a spectator. If you have a mind
to exercise or show your judgment, do it in playing
your own game, when you have an opportunity, not
in criticising or meddling with, or counseling the
play of others.

Lastly. If the game is not to be played vigorously,
according to the rules above mentioned, then mod-
erate your desire for victory over your adversary,
and be pleased with one over yourself. Snatch not
eagerly at every advantage offered by his unskilful-
ness or inattention; but point out to him kindly that
by such a move he places or leaves a piece in danger
or unsupported, that by another he will put his king
in danger, etc. By this generous civility (so opposite
to the unfairness above forbidden) you may indeed
happen to lose the game to your opponent, but you
will win what is better, his esteem, his respect and
his affection; together with the silent approbation
and good will of impartial spectators.

BOOK REVIEW.

"Abridgment of the Law," by Nicholas Statham,
translated by Margaret Center Klingelsmith, LL.B.
('98 L., University of Pennsylvania), Librarian of
the Biddle Law Library, University of Pennsylvania. Boston: The Boston Book Company, 1915.

Two handsome quarto volumes of 1,308 pages, illustrated by two reproductions of the curiously abridged
Latin and French text of the original, printed about
1470, with a foreword of acknowledgment to the University of Pennsylvania and a dedication to William
Draper Lewis, are the ripe fruit of many years of
study. The Introduction, of twenty-three pages, is an
admirable summary of the points that make this
venerable book of value as one of the sources of the
history of English Law, and an intimate knowledge
of the literature of the subject is shown in the notes
scattered through the many pages. Now first translated, the publishers have given it a type and paper
worthy of the learning and industry both of the ancient author and the modern editor. It will take its
place in the "Memorial Library of the Publications
of the University of Pennsylvania and Her Sons" as
the work of one of its students. In the Foreword
Mrs. Klingelsmith ascribes the inspiration to the task
so well executed by William Draper Lewis, long and
until lately the Dean, and still Professor of the Law
Department of the University of Pennsylvania; and
to the University she says, with touching humility,
"I owe all the requirements that have enabled me to
do the work at all," but the debt has long been paid
by her years of good service as Librarian of the
Biddle Law Library, and by her success in acquiring
for it many of the early law books that enrich its
shelves. Not only is hers the first translation of a
book used and mentioned by every writer on English
Law from Coke and Littleton, but down to Pollock
and Maitland. George F. Deiser, a graduate of the
University and one of its first Gowen Fellows, is the
first to translate the earliest of the Year Books, thus
winning the honor of publication by the Selden
Society, the most important agency for giving modern
dress to the venerable sources of English Law. There
remains only one English Law Book, Fleta, to be
translated, and it is to be hoped that either Mrs.
Klingelsmith or Mr. Deiser or some other graduate
of the Law Department will accomplish that task and
thereby add to the credit of the University. To the
Boston Book Company and to its head, Mr. Frank
Ellsworth Chipman, Mrs. Klingelsmith makes grate-
ful acknowledgment of her appreciation of the value
to the legal world, of a translation of Statham.

The dress given to these stately volumes by the
publishers and the printers is of itself a tribute to the
laborious task so well accomplished by the scholarly
editor in the faithful text and the illuminative notes.
No doubt the University will, in due time, recommend
that a suitable honorary degree be conferred on Mrs.
Klingelsmith, to be added to the modest LL.B. now
belonging to her. In this way the University will
give due recognition to her long years of active usefulness in and for the Library, and to the research,
scholarship and literary industry exhibited in her
translation of Statham's Abridgment and the learned
Preface and notes.—J. G. Rosengarten.

STATHAM'S ABRIDGMENT AND ITS TRANSLATOR.

Mrs. Margaret Center Klingelsmith, the translator of Statham's Abridgment, which has just been published, and a review of which appears in this issue, was born in New England and was graduated from the Law School in 1898. Only two women had graduated from the University of Pennsylvania Law School up to that time. She was one of the best students in her class, received honors during the course, and honorable mention for her essay on the Common Law.

From 1896 to 1898 she was assistant librarian, and to write numerous articles on Constitutional Law, which have received special approbation. Her articles on the Common Law have been copied in legal periodicals the world over.

The study of the ancient Norman French and other black letter volumes by the necessity of translating them for users of library books in black letter type in various languages, for which there had never been any translations, led her to specialize along these lines. For the past fifteen years she has been engaged in reading and translating the more difficult of the early law books in Norman French and other languages, and in the translation of manuscripts and the study of paleography and the various early court

Quare incubrauit

SAMPLE OF TEXT REPRODUCED FROM THE ORIGINAL STATHAM'S ABRIDGMENT.

since that time librarian of the Biddle Law Library of the University. During her administration this library has increased from ten thousand to almost fifty-seven thousand volumes, so that it is now one of the largest and best collections of law books in America. Several times she has been sent abroad by the University of Pennsylvania on various missions. In 1904 and in 1910 she collected for the University throughout England rare books for the Biddle Library, principally on the sources of English Law, in which the Library is now exceptionally rich. Mrs. Klingelsmith is not only a lawyer and a great librarian, but is one of the foremost legal writers. To Lewis's "Great American Lawyers" she contributed biographies of James Wilson and Jeremiah Sullivan Black. The former was especially highly praised by the press. Study of the life of James Wilson, member of the Constitutional Convention of 1787, led her

hands. Mrs. Klingelsmith is perhaps the only woman in the United States capable of reading and translating this material; indeed there are but few scholars in the United States capable of doing it. These texts are rendered additionally difficult because of the many phrases, abbreviations of words, etc., peculiar to the times.

Since 1911 she has been engaged upon translating an Abridgment edited by Sir Nicholas Statham, which had never before been translated, and which was printed in a very beautiful but obscure type with many abbreviations not used in ordinary black letter books, requiring a knowledge of paleography. Since the English Year Books had not then been printed the citations in these volumes were incomplete, and no paging could be given. The citations of the Year Books have been added by Mrs. Klingelsmith with much labor and patience. She has also written many notes to the subjects where the historical knowledge of the subject was incomplete.

Mrs. Klingelsmith is not only a scholar and scientist, but a woman who keeps up with many phases of national politics, municipal affairs, and various modern political and social problems. She is a member of the Executive Board of the Alumnae of the University of Pennsylvania, vice-president of the Women Lawyers' Association for Pennsylvania, vice-president of the Women's Democratic Club of Pennsylvania, and an ardent suffrage worker. She is a descendant, both directly and collaterally, of one of the Mayflower families, who settled in Massachusetts in 1620.

The book known as Statham's Abridgment, referred to above, is accredited to Nicola Statham, generally supposed to have been created Baron of the Exchequer, but there is no certainty that he ever received that appointment. His Abridgment is, however, the earliest of the common law ever printed. It was published by Tailleur and Rouen, as the colophon shows, and printed for "R. Redman," one of the earliest of English publishers of law books. The type is one not known to have been used in England, and the book may have been printed in Rouen and sent to England or the type may have been taken to England and set up there. It is a very beautiful type, preserving in an interesting way many of the peculiarities of the written books of the period immediately preceding the introduction of printing, including some of the abbreviations so frequent in manuscript work. The frequency of these abbreviations and their arbitrary nature, while not interfering with the use of the book at the time of its printing, since its clear and beautiful type was a great improvement upon even the best manuscripts in point of legibility, for the manuscripts were even more freely abbreviated, after some time led to the restriction of the use of the book to the more learned. In the course of time as the learning required for the use of the book became less and less common, it became the custom to refer to it as a book which had been superseded by the later abridgments, and as even those who still used the Year Books found it difficult to read Statham's print, they came to depend upon the later Abridgments of Fitzherbert and Brooke, whose print and language were more like those of the Year Books. In the end the Abridgment came to be spoken of in this way: It is Fuller of the "Worthies" speaking of Statham; "His book is much esteemed for the antiquity thereof, for otherwise lawyers hold him as soldiers do bows and arrows, rather for sight than service."

Since Fuller's time all law libraries have felt it to be their duty to acquire a copy of the abridgment, and even of late to pay high prices for one, but few regarded it as of any practical use. Yet the abridgment is the forerunner of the long line of abridgments and digests which are still appearing in ever increasing numbers. It was, as has been said, the earliest of all such works to be printed, as it appeared somewhere between 1470 and 1475, so far as can now be judged. It was before the days of title pages, and bears no date or introductory matter, having only a list of titles before the matter itself. Its classification has been followed in many ways from that day to this, and while many of the titles now speak only of matters unknown to the older law, many others are still to be found in the Abridgments of to-day. It contains many cases not in Brooke and Fitzherbert, and classifies the law as it appeared to a member of the bar a generation before the appearance of the next great abridgment, that of Sir Anthony Fitzherbert. The usefulness of the book became apparent as a new generation of searchers after the truth in the law appeared, who were no longer content to take the word of the earlier writers at second hand. The teacher and the student, and in rare cases, the practitioner, went back to the Year Books themselves in search for authority, and as a part of the Year Book learning, to those abridgments to which citations appeared on the pages of the later editions of the Year Books. These abridgments were only three in number, and were those of Statham, Fitzherbert and Brooke, and of these Statham was the earliest; the original worker. But comparatively few could read Statham with the ease required for a quick reference; some slight knowledge of paleography being now required of those who would read him correctly. The undergraduate student could not be referred to a book he had not had time to learn to read; the busy lawyer could not find time to learn to read him. Therefore it seemed to some who believe in going to the sources of things that the earliest abridgment of the law of the English-speaking world should no longer be a matter of "sight rather than service," but that it had an important service to render to the student of the law. For that reason the work was done. The original is a rather small folio, or, more properly speaking, a tall quarto, of some 187 folios or 374 pages. To the average lawyer it would appear an impossible task to translate it and complete the references to the Year Books so as to render them available to the student, and even to this great scholar it proved to be a work of more than five years. Patience more than any other virtue was needed, and a good deal of patience must have been used before the end of the work was in sight, for it proved to need two large volumes and more than twelve hundred pages for the translation of the entire work, and the few notes added by Mrs. Klingelsmith do not greatly increase the bulk of the work. They were made necessary to explain the matter for that part of the text which has grown somewhat obscure in the passing of the centuries.—G. E. Nitzsche.

IMPROVING THE ALUMNI DAY PARADE.

Suggestions for a Historical Pageant.

Since the Alumni Day Parade at the University seems to have become an annual feature of University life in West Philadelphia, just as much so as the New Year's Pageant has become a permanent institution of the city, it seems that steps might well be taken each year to make the "Parade" original and distinctive. Those who have served on committees in charge of such affairs can fully appreciate the many difficulties which confront those who do the actual work, not the least of which is the lack of funds. With little effort and with not much more expense, however, the Alumni Day Parade might be greatly improved and transformed into a beautiful University of Pennsylvania pageant, which would attract more alumni, their families and friends from all parts of the country. It would have the additional advantage of impressing the alumni, students and the public with the early historical facts and the important part which the sons of the University of Pennsylvania took in those events. For instance, instead of so many of the classes appearing in comic costumes such as clowns, cowboys, devils, Indians, convicts, tramps, etc., which are all very well in their way and which cause considerable amusement, it might be better to have less of this and more classes in historic costumes or on class floats representing historical incidents.

The history of the University, like that of the city, affords innumerable opportunities for a pageant which would not only be original and have an educational value, but which would be beautiful and artistic in itself. As with the city, enough history is made and enough achieved at the University each year in these progressive times to show, by means of floats and pageants, that she is more than keeping abreast of the times. The alumni should take advantage of these opportunities on occasions such as Alumni Day.

Some of the ideas here expressed suggested themselves to the writer a few days ago, when he proposed to a representative of the 1901 Medical Class to urge the members of his class, when celebrating their fifteenth reunion next June, to appear in the Alumni Day Parade in costumes similar to the one worn by John Morgan, who founded the Medical School in 1765—such costume to be patterned after the picturesque Colonial suit in which Morgan was accoutred when the eminent Angelica Kauffman painted the portrait which now hangs on the walls of the Medical School. In 1914, when the Class of 1904 College presented to the University the statue of Benjamin Franklin the members of the class appeared in costumes similar to the one worn by Benjamin Franklin at the French court. This was by far the most effective and artistic attempt that had ever been made by a University class in any of the Alumni Day Parades. There are other University characters who might thus be memorialized in an Alumni Day Pageant. One of the Law Classes, for instance, might wear costumes modeled after the Rosenthal painting of Justice James Wilson, who founded the Law School in 1790. A class in the College might adopt the costume of William Smith, the first Provost of the University, using as a model the painting by Benjamin West, which represents the Provost in a black gown and white stole.

Among the signers of the Declaration of Independence were ten men who were connected with the University of Pennsylvania. A float reproducing this scene from Trumbull's painting, with the University of Pennsylvania representatives in the foreground, would be of great interest. Another subject might be that of John Nixon, a trustee of the University, who in 1776 read and proclaimed the Declaration of Independence publicly for the first time from a platform in Independence Square. Another float might depict Peter Muhlenberg, 1763 College, the fighting parson, as he appeared while delivering a sermon before a large congregation, when he took off his clerical robe, disclosing a colonel's uniform under it, and in this picturesque fashion entered the Colonial army. This might be reproduced from the Muhlenberg statue now in front of City Hall. Still another float might represent Colonel Tench Tilghman, 1761 College, in his ride from Yorktown, Va., when he carried the message of the surrender of Cornwallis for General Washington to Congress, then assembled in Philadelphia. Many of the discoveries made by University of Pennsylvania men might also be the subject of floats, such as the discovery of the blow pipe by Hare, the early experiments in moving-pictures by Muybridge, the first use of ether as an anæsthetic by Long.

Among historical incidents which might be reproduced on Alumni Day, and which would also make appropriate subjects for mural decorations for University halls are following: The imprisonment of William Smith, the first Provost of the University, when he delivered lectures to his classes from the prison window of the old jail at Third and Market Streets, where he was incarcerated by some spiteful action on the part of one of the early Assemblies. Another is the meeting of the Board of Trustees of the "Academy" (afterwards the University of Pennsylvania), held on November 13, 1749, when the copy of the "Constitutions" was signed by James Logan, Thomas Lawrence, William Allen, John Inglis, Tench Francis, William Masters, Lloyd Zachary, Samuel McCall, Jr., Joseph Turner, Benjamin Franklin, Thomas Leech, William Shippen, Robert Strettell, Philip Syng, Charles Willing, Phineas Bond, Richard Peters, Abraham Taylor, Thomas Bond, Thomas Hopkinson, William Plumstead, Joshua Maddox, Thomas White, and William Coleman. This was the first meeting at which a number of important things were accomplished, and the meeting at which Benjamin Franklin was elected president. Since all of these men were prominent citizens and distinguished professional men, with Benjamin Franklin presiding, the group would be an interesting one. Oil paintings of many of the members of this Board are still in existence.

At the meeting just mentioned one of the provisions in the "Constitutions," which had already appeared in Franklin's "Proposals" and to which all of the men in question affixed their signatures, was: "It is hoped and expected that the Trustees will make it their pleasure, and in some degree their business, to visit the Academy often, encourage and countenance the youth, countenance and assist the masters, and by all means in their power advance the usefulness and reputation of the design; that they look on the students as in some sort their children, treat them with familiarity and affection, and when they have behaved well and have gone through their studies and are to enter the world, zealously unite to make all the interest that can be made to establish them, whether in business, offices, marriages, or any other thing for their advantage, preferably to all other persons whatsoever, even of equal merit" (a difficult task for 24 trustees with 8,000 students in 1916). After 1751, when the Academy was opened this group of Trustees did interest themselves in the students of the Academy as provided. This suggestion would give the pageant master or the artist an opportunity of using Franklin and the various distinguished Trustees, with reproductions of interiors and exteriors of the original buildings and students in various activities.

Another incident which might be portrayed is the opening ceremony of the Academy, which took place on January 7, 1851, and which somewhere is described as follows: "Yesterday being the day appointed for the opening of the Academy in this city, the Trustees met and waited on his Honor, our Governor, to the public hall of the building where the Rev. Mr. Peters made an excellent sermon on the occasion to a crowded audience."

A reproduction of the first Commencement exercises, held on May 17, 1757, when Provost Smith delivered the address to the six graduates of the first class, consisting of Duche, Hopkinson, Latta, Magaw, Morgan, and Williamson.

The Commencement exercises of May 10, 1775, which were attended by George Washington and the members of the Continental Congress, would also make a most impressive picture. This Commencement was described in a newspaper of that time as being held "in the presence of the most illustrious assembly this Seminary ever beheld. About half an hour after nine o'clock, agreeable to an invitation previously given them, the honorable members of the Continental Congress were pleased to proceed in a body from the State House to the College, where they were received at the gates by the Provost, Vice-Provost, professors, graduates, and other students in their proper habits; they entered the hall and took their places, the galleries and other parts of the house being filled with as many of the respectable inhabitants of the city as could find room." This would enable the artist or pageant master to portray a picturesque outdoor procession, with the officers and faculty in their academic gowns, the members of Congress in Colonial dress. Since Benjamin Franklin was a member of the Continental Congress, having just returned from London in the spring of 1775, both Washington and Franklin might be included in the procession. This would enable the old Academy buildings and Provost Smith's house to be used as a background.—G. E. Nitzsche.

UNIVERSITY OF PENNSYLVANIA CLUB OF NEW YORK CITY.

Banquet at the Hotel McAlpin, Saturday Evening, February 5.

The University of Pennsylvania men of New York City and vicinity announce that their twenty-eighth annual dinner will be held at the Hotel McAlpin, Broadway and Thirty-fourth Street, on Saturday evening, February 5, 1916, at 7 o'clock, under the auspices of the University of Pennsylvania Club of New York City.

The announcement of the club states that this is the one annual function which every son of Pennsylvaia should strive to attend, not merely to partake of a most excellent dinner with old college friends, but to replenish the spirit of loyalty to Alma Mater, and, by his presence, contribute to the formation of an assemblage that will be commensurate with the importance of our University.

A seating schedule is to be printed and men in attendance will be seated at tables by classes and then by professions or departments, unless specific instructions to the contrary are given the committee.

No attempt will be made to assign seats for those men whose acceptances reach the committee's hands later than Friday morning, February 4, although unclassified tables will be provided to accommodate all late-comers.

Tables may be reserved for parties of eight or more.

The charge for this dinner is three dollars and a half ($3.50) per plate for Pennsylvania men and their guests.

Bring as many guests as you desire. Why not get up a party of eight and have your own table?

Send your acceptance without delay, on an "Acceptance" blank, with funds, to E. C. Kindleberger, Chairman, Room 1608, Municipal Building, New York City—then, urge your classmates to do likewise.

Make checks payable to "William Guggenheim, Treasurer."

As usual, a large and active reception committee will greet every man as he reaches the dining hall and will introduce the men at each table to one another and endeavor to make all feel at home.

The speakers will discuss this year questions of the day as well as matters relating to our University.

Hon. John Barrett, formerly United States Minister to the Argentine Republic, Panama and Colombia, and at present Director-General of the Pan-American Union, will speak on "Pan-Americanism—America's Greatest Present-Day Opportunity."

Hon. George Haven Putnam, the well-known publisher and author, and late Brevet-Major 176th Regiment, N. Y. S. Vols., will speak on "The Defence of the Republic and the Fulfilment of our National Obligations."

Provost Edgar F. Smith will give an address about "The University."

Hugh W. Ogden, Esq., newly elected president of the Associated Pennsylvania Clubs, will discuss the important work of that organization.

John H. Minds, Esq., one of the members of the Football Committee of the Athletic Association, will speak about "Athletics."

Severo Mallet-Prevost, Esq., who was so successful last year as Toastmaster, will again assume that important duty.

The Dinner Committee includes: William Blaney, William B. Boulton, Fenwick Beekman, M.D., C. N. B. Camac, M.D., L. C. Curtis, Erskine B. Essig, Frank R. Ford, William Guggenheim, Charles C. Grant, G. W. Hobby, D.D.S., Percival Hill, Arthur C. Johnson, Jr., Charles P. Krieg, William McClellan, Samuel McCullagh, M.D., Samuel K. Probasco, William A. Redding, John R. Savage, Rev. William J. Thompson, Henry G. Ward, Everett W. Warfield, Harrison B. Weil; E. Crosby Kindleberger, Chairman, Room 1608, Municipal Building, New York City.

BOOK REVIEWS.

Good English—a Practical Manual of Correct Speaking and Writing. By John L. Haney, '98 Col., '01 Grad., Professor of English Philology, Philadelphia Central High School. Cloth bound, 244 pages. The Edgerton Press, Philadelphia, Pa., 1915.

This book is a convenient reference work that discusses more than a thousand words and phrases occurring often in colloquial speech. By following the dictionary plan of presenting the articles in alphabetical order Dr. Haney has facilitated the use of this book and has made its information immediately available for the most inexperienced reader. The text has been cleared as far as possible of the technical expressions of grammar, so that the explanations may be more readily understood.

The book is likewise, we believe, well adapted to the needs of English teachers in colleges and high schools. Its use should accomplish the practical result of correcting for the student those errors and colloquialisms that now occasion widespread criticism of the results obtained in following prevailing methods of English training. To students in business colleges who are preparing for careers in which a knowledge of good English is essential, the book should prove itself particularly helpful.

Dr. Haney has done much valuable work in English and is also the author of a number of other English works, among which are "A Bibliography of S. T. Coleridge," "Early Reviews of English Poets," "The Name of Wm. Shakespeare," etc.

UNIVERSITY EXTENSION WORK IN AMERICA HAD ITS ORIGIN AT THE UNIVERSITY OF PENNSYLVANIA.

Written for "Old Penn" and the "Public Ledger," by George Henderson, '89 C., '96 L.

An interesting article in a recent issue of the Philadelphia "Ledger" describes the New York City course of lectures as "not mere lectures," but a real university, recalls the large part which the University of Pennsylvania and Philadelphia had in initiating the movement for University Extension in this country; and it suggests the opportunity for developing in Philadelphia and throughout Pennsylvania urban universities, and by urban universities I mean those which will fill the needs of the whole community and which will strive to maintain in the field of higher education equality of opportunity for the whole people.

The University Extension movement was started by Cambridge University, England, in 1873. The inception of this movement was not entirely democratic. Dr. Pusey tells us that it had its inception in the thought that Cambridge and Oxford should be doing something for the masses of people and thereby protecting these old institutions from a meddling Parliament.

Through the fall of 1889 Dr. William Pepper, then Provost of the University of Pennsylvania, called a series of conferences looking towards the starting of University Extension in Philadelphia and finally in June, 1890, there was organized the Philadelphia Society for University Extension. Among those associated with Provost Pepper in this effort were Frederick B. Miles, who became the first Treasurer of the Society; the writer, who became the first General Secretary; Samuel Wagner, a nephew of the founder of the Wagner Free Institute of Science; Mrs. Matthew Baird, Mrs. William Hunt, Mrs. Caspar Wistar, President Isaac Sharpless, Rev. Dr. John S. MacIntosh, Charles E. Bushnell, and Talcott Williams.

For a number of years previously the University of Pennsylvania, through the University Lecture Association, had given annually a series of scholarly lectures. This lecture Association was later merged into the Philadelphia Society, which afterwards was expanded into the American Society for University Extension. The aim of the Society was democratic and cultural.

In the fall of 1889 the University Lecture Association had invited to this city Prof. Richard G. Moulton, who for many years had been one of the most successful lecturers in the Cambridge University Extension. Professor Moulton's enthusiasm and zeal for this broader field of education were great aids in starting the movement in this country.

After the American Society was organized the Secretary was sent to England to study their plans and methods, and in the fall of 1890 the work was started in and around Philadelphia. The first organized, systematic Extension Course given in the United States was at St. Timothy's Workmen's Club and Institute in Roxborough, and was delivered by Prof. C. Hanford Henderson on chemistry.

During the first year more than twenty-five thousand attended these University Extension lectures and the following year an even greater number. Centers were organized throughout Pennsylvania, New

Jersey, Delaware, Maryland, and some courses we delivered in New York and Connecticut.

At the outset the methods developed in **England** this work were followed here, but it was felt th eventually the movement would adapt itself American conditions and the way in which it h done so is interesting.

. Chautauqua had been striving for some **years** democratize higher education and in 1890 whe Bishop Vincent was abroad he made a special stud of the University Extension Movement in Englan He wrote home to Dr. William R. Harper, who wa associated with him in the Chautauqua work, sendin him a description of the University Extension Move ment and suggesting that he should at once secur several lecturers and start the work so that Chautau qua should have the credit of inaugurating Universit; Extension in America.

The plans, however, of Provost Pepper were so fa: developed that before Dr. Harper could do anything the work was well started in and around Philadelphia and thus to the City of Brotherly Love and the Uni versity of Pennsylvania belongs the credit of starting in the United States the movement for democracy in higher education—a movement which is reforming our universities and bids fair to have a far-reaching influence on the form and content of higher educa tion.

While Philadelphia started the movement for de mocracy in higher education it remained for Chicago to take the next great strides in advance, and it should be remarked in passing that these steps forward were taken under the direction of a Philadelphian, President Harper, of the University of Chicago, who had been implored to remain at Yale and semi-officially had been promised the presidency in succession to President Timothy Dwight, had in the spring of 1892 persuaded the General Secretary of University Extension in Philadelphia to become the Director of the University Extension Division of the University of Chicago. From that institution went forth the first efforts for University Extension in Illinois, Indiana, Ohio, Michigan, Wisconsin, Iowa, and Minnesota.

Three forward steps were taken by the University of Chicago (1) Correspondence Teaching; (2) a Summer Term of the University; and (3) extra mural classes.

(1) Correspondence Teaching. For some years previous to accepting the Presidency of the University of Chicago, while Professor of Hebrew at Yale, Dr. Harper, through his Institute of Sacred Literature, had conducted correspondence teaching. This work was largely among ministers, both young and old, and among those preparing for a career in the ministry. The method was by correspondence. Lessons sheets gave an outline of a course of study, with a bibliography of collateral reading. At the end of the course an examination was frequently held under the direction of some one who could vouch for its integrity.

Such teaching never will take the place of the living present teacher, and President Harper never claimed it would. It has, however, proved a great aid to those who were in earnest and were so situated that they could get nothing better.

The University of Chicago was the first to offer systematic instruction in many fields by correspondence and tens of thousands have benefited thereby.

(2) A Summer Term of the University. Many institutions had been holding Summer Schools, which

were early looked upon askance; they were tolerated, but few thought of them as offering scholarly results.

President Harper saw great possibilities in them; he realized that for the most part they were composed of serious students in quest of aid for practical ends. He therefore divided the year into four University terms and made the Summer Term—July, August and September—co-ordinate with any of the other terms. The student may take a full course during the Summer Term, or less, depending entirely upon his capacity.

The summer student is no longer lightly regarded; he has demonstrated his seriousness of purpose and the high grade of his work. Formerly his work was so lightly regarded that no mention was made of it in the various University reports. This is all changed to-day. The last report of the University of Pennsylvania shows that out of a total enrollment of 8,069, no less than 1,035 were in the Summer School; at Columbia University, out of 17,016, no less than 5,590 were in the Summer School.

The development of the summer session has been a very great step forward in democratizing higher education.

(3) Extra Mural Classes. These were first offered in a systematic way by the University of Chicago when it opened in the fall of 1892. They were then practically the Freshmen and Sophomore Courses given by the faculty in convenient units, at convenient hours and places for those so situated that they could not attend the regular courses on the campus of the University. Their grade was assured by the fact that they were given by the University faculty. The first class to be organized was one in Latin conducted by Professor Willis Gardner Hale, the Head Professor in that subject in the University, and was very largely attended.

Extra mural classes were established shortly afterwards by the University of Pennsylvania, and are conducted not only in Philadelphia, but in most of the larger cities of the State. The grade of this work is so high that University credit is awarded for it. The University Catalogue reports 2,494 as attending these classes, while at Columbia University the number is 5,152. Teachers have profited very largely by these courses.

It can therefore be stated with confidence that academic work of a high grade can be successfully carried on upon Saturdays, in the evening, in the summer, at convenient places, for the benefit of those who cannot command their whole time in going to college.

Our universities and colleges are face to face with the problem of academic education for the masses for their vocations and for life. Culture, in the old-fashioned sense, is largely still reserved for the classes; but we should remember what President Nicholas Murray Butler said a few years ago to the effect that any culture which survived in this democratic age would be of a very matter-of-fact, bread-and-butter kind.

The time was when some very eminent persons held the view that the masses were not capable of higher education. For a long time we have been impounding huge reservoirs of knowledge; it will be of little use to add to these unless there are ways found for disseminating this knowledge among the masses and rendering it productive. President Van Hise has remarked that were our present knowledge of medicine properly disseminated, disease could be cut in half; and in the same way a dissemination of our knowledge of agriculture would probably double the productions of the soil.

But how is this problem of academic education for the masses to be solved? Existing agencies are not adequate to cope with it. The first step is frankly to recognize and face the situation; then a sympathetic attitude towards the issues involved will greatly aid in discovering the forward steps necessary to a solution.

BOOK REVIEWS.

"A Student's History of Education," by Frank Pierrepont Graves, Ph.D., Dean of the School of Education and Professor of the History of Education, University of Pennsylvania. New York: Macmillan Company, 1915, pp. 453.

Few text-books in any field of knowledge have received the enthusiastic reception that has been given Professor Graves' "Student's History of Education." The first edition of nine thousand was sold within a month after publication, and a second has been almost entirely exhausted. It is already in use in between four and five hundred educational institutions, including nine of the normal schools and a dozen of the colleges of Pennsylvania. It has been translated into Spanish, German and French, and been favorably reviewed in a multitude of journals. Perhaps the most striking characterization of it has been made by the Professor of Philosophy in an important western institution who calls it "the rare kind of book which would set the teacher at liberty." Naturally, what appeals most to me personally is its unusual efficiency from a pedagogical point of view, especially the compact outline with which each chapter begins.

To quote from the foreword: "By having this outline in mind when he studies the facts, the student is enabled not only to see that the general statements are verified and made more significant by the details, but at the same time to organize the facts with reference to the generalization, and thereby secure an easier control of them, and, through the relation of each to the others, discover a fuller meaning in them all. Then, after this study of the details has established the truth of the outline and enriched its meaning, he can review the outline and fix it in mind as the conclusion of the chapter."

As Professor Birch, of Wittenberg College, well says:

This outline, "the organization of each chapter, the topics along the margin, the bibliography at the end of each chapter, and the picking out of essential facts make the book the most workable, thorough and comprehensive now on the market."

Other representative critics refer to its "concreteness," its "clearness and directness of style," its "well selected illustrations" and its "adaptation to introductory courses through an emphasis of the modern educational movement which is at the same time organically connected with the older periods."

With all of these comments I feel myself in hearty accord, with an added feeling of pride in the fact that a friend and colleague has written what one of the greatest college presidents and educational leaders in America has called "the most readable and usable book on the history of education, in one volume, that has yet been published."

A. DUNCAN YOCUM.

527

THE LATIN DEPARTMENT'S COLLECTION OF ANTIQUITIES.

III. MIRRORS.

By Dr. John C. Rolfe,
Professor of the Latin Language and Literature.

Among the most interesting objects in the collection are two bronze mirrors from Etruria, one of which is in an unusually perfect state of preservation, while the other, although somewhat damaged, is of

from place to place and used more conveniently and more constantly, was an easy and obvious one, which would be suggested by seeing the reflection of one's face in polished armor or in household utensils.

The most usual material of the extant ancient mirrors is bronze, although silver mirrors are by no means uncommon. We hear of their being made also of gold or even of gems, and Seneca ("Naturales Quæstiones," 1, 17, 9) asserts that in his time freedmen's daughters often spent more money on a single mirror than the sum which the senate voted as a

Ancient Mirrors and Mirror-Cases.

Figs. 5 and 6. Egyptian Mirrors in the University Museum.

Fig. 7. Greek Box-Mirror, with Aphrodite Pandemos.

Figs. 8 and 9. Greek Box-Mirror, with incised decoration inside.

Fig. 10. Archaic Mirror from Etruria, with decoration in relief.

Fig. 11. Greek Standing Mirror, from Corinth.

Fig. 12. Archaic Greek Standing Mirror, from Athens.

Fig. 13. Pear-shaped Mirror from Praeneste, made in one piece.

Etruscan Mirrors in the Collection of the Latin Department.

The Mirror from Fidenae, with Peleus and Thetis: Fig. 1, photograph; Fig. 2, line drawing.

The Mirror from Fescennium, with the Cabeiri: Fig. 3, photograph; Fig. 4, line drawing.

particular interest because of the scene represented upon it.

The need of a mirror of some kind must have been felt by mankind at a very early period and was probably first met by resorting to the surface of a smooth sea, to a quiet stream or pool, or to a polished rock. Thus Ovid, in his "Metamorphoses" (xiii, 839 f.), represents the amorous Cyclops Polyphemus as saying:

Certe ego me novi liquidaeque in imagine vidi
Nuper aquae, placuitque mihi mea forma videnti.

The next step, to provide a polished surface of metal for this purpose, which could be transported

dowry for the daughters of Scipio Africanus, the conqueror of Hannibal. But, as might be expected, none of these costly specimens has survived to our day.

Mirrors of bronze were used in remote antiquity by the Egyptians, and our Free Museum of Science and Art has some good examples (Figs. 5, 6). These all correspond with those shown in illustrated books on Egypt and with specimens in other museums in having an oblate form, a shape which is not found elsewhere and which seems to be characteristic of the native Egyptian mirrors. The mirrors found in Egypt in Roman times are circular, like the greater number of those which have been discovered in

Greece and Italy. The Egyptian mirrors were provided with spikes, by means of which a handle of wood, ivory, bone, or metal could be attached. In many cases the handles were of the same material as the mirrors themselves, but they appear always to have been made separately and attached in the manner described. The handles were almost always ornamented, sometimes elaborately, but the mirrors themselves are without decoration of any kind, although in rare instances they bear inscriptions. Even the inscriptions, however, when they occur at all, are for the most part inscribed on the handles.

Metal mirrors were unquestionably known to the Greeks at an early period of their history, although the number of specimens which have been preserved is relatively small compared with the great quantity found in Etruria. They are mentioned in the Homeric poems, but since handsomely ornamented mirrors of great antiquity have been found at Mycenae, Euripides seems to be guilty of no anachronism in putting mirrors into the hands of the Trojan dames, even though they be golden ones. The Greek mirrors differ from those of Egypt in their shape, in the addition of ornamentation to the mirror disc itself, and apparently also in a greater variety of style. Besides the ordinary hand-mirror of the conventional form, we have standing mirrors, some of which could also be held in the hand; round mirrors without handles, the so-called "orbes"; square mirrors, like those found at Pompeii, and numerous other varieties.

The Greeks also seem to have been the first to make the so-called box-mirrors, in which the reflecting surface is protected by being on the inside of a case. Some specimens (Fig. 7) have a handle for lifting the lid and a projection at the top, apparently for hanging up the mirror when it was not in use. The beautiful relief on this mirror-case represents Aphrodite Pandemos, after the celebrated statue by Scopas, which is also reproduced on coins of Elis. Although this mirror is said to have been found in Palestrina, it is unquestionably of Greek workmanship, as are also some of those which have been found in Etruria. In some instances not only was the cover ornamented with work in relief, but the inside of the box had an incised design as well (Figs. 8, 9). The reflecting surface was in such cases, and apparently always, on the inside of the cover, so that in the hinged variety at least the bottom of the box might serve as a support when the mirror was open and in use.

Figs. 11, 12 show two characteristic specimens of the Greek standing mirrors. Of these, the more archaic of the two (Fig. 12) is from Athens, and the other from Corinth. Each is ornamented on the edge with two figures of Eros, while the handle is in each instance a statuette of Aphrodite.

In Italy mirrors have so far been found mainly in three localities: in Etruria, and for the most part southern Etruria; Palestrina, the ancient Praeneste, and Pompeii. Etruria has yielded more than a thousand specimens. The mirrors which can with certainty be assigned to Rome are few and unimportant, although box-mirrors with relief medallions of Roman emperors have been found in various parts of the Italian peninsula and in the provinces. Pliny tells us in his "Natural History" (33, 130) that mirrors of silver were first made in the time of Pompey the Great, a statement which obviously can apply only to Italy; but in another passage he says that by his time silver mirrors had become so common that even maid servants owned them.

Mirrors of glass were unquestionably known in ancient times, and within recent years a considerable number of specimens has been found. They were never so popular, however, as those of metal, and they never seem to have reached a high degree of perfection. The use of mercury as a backing does not seem to have been known in antiquity, and the general use of glass mirrors seems not to antedate the twelfth century.

Besides the small hand-mirrors and standing mirrors, large wall-mirrors were known to both the Greeks and the Romans. Vitruvius ("Architecture," 9, 9, 2) tells us of a barber's son of Alexandria, Ctesibius by name, who was led to the invention of hydraulic machines by attempting to arrange in the paternal tonsorial parlors a large wall-mirror, which could be raised or lowered at will. Both Seneca ("Naturales Quaestiones," 1, 17, 8) and Ulpian ("Digest," 34, 2, 19, 8) speak of mirrors large enough to show the whole figure at once, and it must have been a mirror of this kind before which Demosthenes is said to have practised. We even hear of entire rooms lined with mirrors.

Magic mirrors of various kinds and properties were known to the ancients, and various forms of divination were practised by means of them. They are frequently (in fact, most frequently) found in tombs, and while the prevailing view at present is that they were deposited there merely as toilet articles, the positions in which they are sometimes found and the magic properties associated with mirrors suggest that they may have had a more intimate connection with burial and with funeral offerings.

Our two specimens are typical Etruscan mirrors, since they are of circular form, and have (or had) handles which were not a part of the mirror, but were made separately and attached to it. The Praenestine mirrors, on the other hand, are ordinarily pear-shaped, and the handle is of one piece with the disc (Fig. 13). Both varieties commonly have designs incised on the back, and this is true of our two examples. A few mirrors are without decoration of any kind, while others have designs in relief, like that of Fig. 10, are rare. In one of our specimens the handle is lost, in the other it is still attached to the mirror and evidently belongs to it, although there are indications that it had become separated from the disc and was attached again in modern times.

The less perfectly preserved, but more interesting specimen of the two (Figs. 1, 2) came from near the site of the ancient Fidenae. While many ancient mirrors are slightly convex and have a raised rim of some height about the engraved side, this one is perfectly flat and has a rim so slight as to be hardly perceptible. The engraving shows one of the scenes from the myth of Peleus and Thetis, the seizure of the goddess by her lover. Thetis is represented with wings, which probably typify her change into a bird in her efforts to avoid capture. Ovid tells us ("Metamorphoses," xi, 243 ff.) that she became successively a bird, a tree and a tigress. The two figures are designated by inscriptions in Greek letters as Thethis and Pele, the regular Etruscan forms of their names.

It is of special interest that this same scene occurs on three, or perhaps four, other mirrors, as well as on an antique representation of a mirror on a lead plate used as the cover of a funeral urn. The genuineness of all of these has been called in question, but there can be no doubt of the authenticity of our mirror, and its discovery seems to support to some extent at least the genuineness of the others.

Our second mirror (Figs. 3, 4), although a much more perfect specimen than the first, is less interesting, and its authenticity, while highly probable, is less certain. It is said to have been found at Calestro, near Civita Castellana, a village which is believed by some to stand on the site of the ancient Fescennium. The mirror is round and perfectly flat, showing no signs of the convexity which is frequently found in extant specimens, as well as in representations of mirrors in works of art. It is unusually thick and heavy, and it has a handle, which is fastened on by some kind of a solder without the use of nails or of a tang of any kind. The handle ends in a ram's head, a common Etruscan decoration.

Unlike the first mirror, this one has a border included between circular lines, which is not quite symmetrical either with reference to the handle or to the scene which it encloses. Strangely enough, too, although the border is a very simple one, it does not occur on any other extant published mirror, which is perhaps an argument in favor of the genuineness of the mirror. The engraving represents a scene which is common in various forms on Etruscan mirrors, consisting of two seated youths with a third standing between them. There are sometimes four figures, and sometimes a temple in the background, a shield, a spear, or some other accessory.

Such groups have been assumed by some to represent scenes in the lives of the Dioscuri, or of the so-called Cabeiri, with whom the Dioscuri were more or less completely identified. According to one legend, there were three Cabeiri, of whom two slew their brother, who was afterwards raised from the dead and deified. Some mirrors are supposed to represent the murderous attack of the two fratricidal brothers, another shows the birth of the three, while groups like ours are assumed to depict the reconciliation of the three brothers after the third has been restored to life. The crown on the head of the standing figure is perhaps indicative of his deification. More recent archaeologists do not attempt to identify the members of these groups, and some even regard them as purely ornamental figures, without special meaning of any kind.

The Arrest of Dr. McCartney at Perugia.

Dr. McCartney, A.B., '06 Ph.D., '11, former Instructor in Latin at the University of Pennsylvania, and now Classical Fellow of the American Academy in Rome, has sent to Professor Rolfe the following account of his arrest at Perugia for "conspiring to blow up the Cathedral with bombs," as was briefly announced in "Old Penn" a few weeks ago:

"As another archaeologist and I were leaving a cafe in Perugia at 3.30 on the fourth day of our visit, the official who had issued our 'permits of sojourn' tapped me on the shoulder and asked me to accompany him to the police office. I knew the request was a command, and so assented with as good grace as possible. Two or three plain-clothes men picked up my companion and off we started.

"On the way my captor asked me, as the arch-conspirator, several questions, the point of which I missed at the time.

" 'Have you been to the Cathedral?'

" 'Yes.'

" 'Does your friend speak Italian?'

" 'Yes; a little.'

" 'Do you talk Italian to each other?'

" 'No.'

" 'You told me that you were going to stay four days. This is the fourth. When do you leave?'

" 'At 5 o'clock.'

"Meanwhile I was trying to think of what sins of omission or commission I had been guilty, but could hit upon nothing except that I had used a vest-pocket kodak at Assisi the day before. Fortunately I had taken it from my pocket and left it in my room only three hours before, since the weather was cloudy.

"At the police office we were asked again for our papers, and our passports were carefully examined. Then came some more questions from another official:

" 'Have you a permit to carry weapons?'

" 'No.'

" 'Have you any weapons?'

" 'No.'

" 'Knives?'

" 'You may search us.'

"He motioned to us to stand up. Then he searched our pockets and felt over our persons, without result, of course.

"At this juncture my first interlocutor, who had satisfied himself about our passports, looked toward the back of the room and said, 'What did you hear?'

"Two small boys of seven or eight years, whom I had not noticed before, stepped forward and said, with great excitement, 'We heard them say that in a little while they would bombard the church with bombs!'

"The humor of the situation was too much for me. My merriment was greater than would ordinarily be tolerated on such an occasion, but fortunately the absurdity of the whole proceeding finally dawned upon the officials, and they laughed, too.

"Until the testimony of the boys I was as much in the dark as you are. Then, however, I suddenly recalled that as we were leaving the Cathedral two youngsters, who had been sitting on the opposite side of a column while we were talking, gave us a peculiar look, but I thought nothing more of it, since many Perugians were suspicious of us. They evidently thought they recognized some of our words, and their imagination had done the rest. It may have been an imagination inspired by the Propertian scenery to which they were accustomed.

"We made no defense against the testimony of the boys except to say that the whole thing was a good joke. We thanked the urchins for the diversion and were dismissed with all the graciousness and courtesy characteristic of the Italian.

"We had no more adventures worthy of note. Being escorted up side alleys and requested to show your papers and being asked if you are 'real Americans' are rather common occurrences.

"Recently an official approached me and said, 'Have you—— ?' I was expecting him to say, 'Have you your passport?' and so missed part of his sentence. Asked to repeat his request, he said 'Have you a match?'

"The experience at Perugia has, however, persuaded me not to make another trip until it is warm enough to spend a night in prison—again, as I did at Naples!"

The Alpha Chapter of Beta Gamma Sigma, a national honorary fraternity for students in commercial courses in American universities, was installed on January 4, in the Wharton School of the University.

UNIVERSITY SERVICES.

Eminent Religious Leaders to Address Students.

During the latter part of January and in February, the following religious leaders of national prominence will visit the University and speak in different churches under the auspices of the Christian Association:

January 16, 11.00 A. M. Central Congregational Church, 18th and Green Streets. Rev. John Douglas Adam, D.D., Professor in Hartford Seminary, Popular Lecturer at Eaglesmere Student Conference. Daily Chapel Speaker from January 17 to 21. 7.45 P. M., Tabernacle Presbyterian Church, 37th and Chestnut Streets, Rev. John Douglas Adam, D.D.

January 23, 11.00 A. M. Tabernacle Presbyterian Church, 37th and Chestnut Streets, Rev. John Douglas Adam, D.D.

January 30, 10.30 A. M. Asbury Methodist Episcopal Church, Chestnut, above 33rd Street. Rev. W. Douglas Mackenzie, D.D., LL.D., President, Hartford Seminary; regular visitor to the University each year; Eaglesmere Conference Speaker.

February 6, 11.00 A. M. St. Mary's Church, Locust, above 39th Street, Rt. Rev. Wilson R. Stearly, D.D., recently consecrated as Bishop Suffragan of Newark, former Rector of the Church of the Holy Apostles. 7.45 P. M., Church of the Saviour, 38th, above Chestnut Street, Rt. Rev. Nathaniel S. Thomas, D.D., Bishop of Wyoming, University Chapel Speaker last year; former Rector of the Church of the Holy Apostles; Christian pioneer on the Western frontier.

February 13, 10.30 A. M., Asbury Methodist Episcopal Church, Chestnut, above 33rd Street, Rev. Harry E. Fosdick, D.D., pastor First Baptist Church, Montclair, N. J.; Professor Union Theological Seminary; author of "The Manhood of the Master"; speaker at Daily Chapel Services, February 14 to 18.

February 20, 10.30 A. M., Chestnut Street Baptist Church, Chestnut, above 40th Street, Rev. Harry E. Fosdick, D.D. 7.45 P. M., Tabernacle Presbyterian Church, 37th and Chestnut Streets, Rev. Harry E. Fosdick, D.D.

February 27, 11.00 A. M. Evangelical Lutheran Church of the Holy Communion, Chestnut, above 21st Street, Rev. John A. W. Haas, D.D., LL.D., President, Muhlenberg College.

Faculty Tea Club.

At the regular meeting of the Faculty Tea Club, Miss Roorbach, Director of Invalid Occupation at the Philadelphia General Hospital, told of her work. At the tea which followed, Mrs. Samuel G. Dixon acted as hostess, with the following ladies assisting: Mrs. David Mitchell, Mrs. C. H. Heuser, Mrs. Alexander Glass, Mrs. F. H. Bohlen, Mrs. Webber, Mrs. W. P. Laird, Mrs. E. M. Patterson, Mrs. J. K. Young, Mrs. R. H. Harte, Mrs. Wm. Pepper, Jr. Mrs. Arthur L. Church presided at the tea table.

Dr. James K. Young Gives a Dinner.

Dr. James K. Young, Associate Professor on Orthopedic Surgery, gave a dinner to those who participated at the meeting of the County Medical Society on December 22, at the University Club. Those present were Dr. R. Tunstall Taylor, of the University of Maryland; Dr. William G. Spiller, Dr. James H. McKee, Dr. Walter G. Elmer, Dr. A. Bruce Gill, Dr. J. T. Rugh and Dr. James K. Young.

BOOK REVIEWS.

"The Great War," by George Henry Allen, A.M., Ph.D., former Assistant in History, University of Pennsylvania, and Captain Henry C. Whitehead, of the United States Army. George Barrie's Sons, Philadelphia.

Among the very many works published and being published concerning the momentous struggle of the world's greatest military forces, this book occupies a distinct place and will be ranked among the permanent contributions to historical literature. The author looks beyond the mere magnitude of the physical forces and the unparalleled operations involved in the titanic struggle, and recognizes that a far greater interest than mere partisanship and sympathy has been quickened throughout the world. He glimpses the profound changes, perhaps the overthrow of present dynasties and governments, the epochal influences on the intellectual, moral, political, social and industrial conditions that are the possible outcome of this appeal to force. He sees the peril involved in the struggle whose shock rocks the interests of the civilized world. He recognizes that the future of democracy is at stake, perhaps imperiled. With such stupendous issues involved, Dr. Allen has set himself the task of disentangling the intricate skein of diplomacy, of tracing the legislation and of noting the sentiment of the nations leading up most directly to and culminating in the fratricidal war. This course has called for a retrospective consideration of the important movements of the nineteenth century "political, social and industrial and the national ambitions and policies" out of which have sprung the immediate causes of the war. He ably discusses the principles of Nationalities and of the Balance of Power, and reviews the territorial adjustments of Europe as the fruit of the struggle between these principles, instances striking violations of the first principle and the consequent unsettlement and retardation of advance in certain states, and its contributory influence on the present war. He briefly traces the unification of Italy and the aspirations of the Irredentists; outlines the causes of Prussia's leadership in Germany and the policy that led to the formation of the present empire. Russia and her numerous heterogeneous peoples are succinctly considered, and the complicated problem of nationalities in Austria-Hungary is shown to be of particular difficulty.

Thus the author, by a general but concise review of national and state adjustments, gives his readers an essential foundation for the comprehension of many of the otherwise mystifying international movements which led more or less surely to the final cataclysm.

He proceeds with a summary examination of the industrial, economical and domestic political situation in the leading belligerent countries.

Dr. Allen next calls up the conspicuous evidences of the substitution of the Kaiser's Welt-politik for Bismarck's solid and conservative foreign policy, and the rapprochement of the two great Central Powers. He reviews some of the more significant movements that grew out of the changed foreign policy of Germany and their bearing upon or creation of the state of suspicion which succeeded in her relations with Great Britain. He sharply designates the conflicting questions that operated to augment Teutonic influence and enfeeble that of Russia and the Western

Powers. Due consideration is given to the Oriental policy of the Kaiser, his singularly aggressive attitude on the Moroccan question, which alarmed Italy and alienated her support and was a powerful factor in the forming of the Triple Entente. He shows how the German people resented the check which the Kaiser's policy suffered in the final settlement of the Moroccan crisis in 1911 and its impulsive force in German policies. This period he regards as a turning point from which events march definitely to the crisis. The author's comprehensive discussion of the Balkan situation is of unusual importance. He makes clear Germany's interest in the States of the Peninsula and shows that her policy required a highway through them to the Dardanelles so that she could develop coveted opportunities in Asia. He establishes the fact that conflict of Teuton and Slav is inevitable, and indicates the steps by which Germany sought to secure commercial supremacy in the Ottoman Empire. He surveys the causes and results of the Balkan war of 1912-13; the disappointment of Austria at the settlement and the extraordinary increase in German military strength that followed Turkey's defeat. He marks the enmity of the Teutonic empires toward Serbia as the great obstacle to their continued expansion; and notes the aspirations of the Slav state toward a greater Serbia and traces the suspicion and ill will that followed her military successes; and the Pan-Slav agitation against Austria that reached its culmination in the assassination of the Archduke Francis Ferdinand in the Bosnian town of Sarajevo, which he visited, in spite of official warning, during the celebration of the almost sacred commemoration of the great Slav defeat at Kosova by the Turks in 1389. He reviews in considerable detail the hesitating course of Austria after this outrage, her sudden, extraordinary and peremptory demand upon Serbia; Germany's effort to confine the settlement of the question to those two powers and her refusal to acquiesce in the proposals of Great Britain and Russia, especially that the issue be considered by outside powers, as involving interests of international moment. The closing hours of diplomatic effort to maintain peace and the consequence of Austria's persistence are reviewed, leading to Russia's mobilization and Germany's ultimatum and declaration of war against her, followed by the abrupt demand of the former upon France and declaration of war, together with the evidence upon which rests the alleged conciliatory last-hour attitude of Austria-Hungary towards Serbia.

The policy of Great Britain in the climactic conflict between Serbia and Austria is unfolded, and that of her anterior policy respecting Belgian neutrality and inviolability; Germany's declaration of war is considered and the ground of the latter's misconception of Great Britain's attitude are examined.

Under the caption, "Was the War Deliberately Provoked?" the author summarizes recent and current military and domestic excitement in Great Britain, Germany and Russia, and furnishes evidence of the artificial conception of military honor and the inimical and dominating spirit it creates.

In the pages covering the participation of the Oriental member of the Entente belligerents, Japan's transformation from a secluded country to a most important world power is sketched vividly, with special reference to her relations with Russia and her course and purpose of alliance with Great Britain;

her later close understanding with Russia; her suspicion of the intentions of Germany, and finally her casting her lot with the enemies of that country. In considering the motives that led Turkey to join the Teutonic power, Dr. Allen demonstrates that such a course was the logical outcome of her recent defeats by the Balkan states and her consequent loss of military power, inasmuch as thereby she hoped most readily to recover some of her lost standing and influence. He points out how Turkey had become enmeshed in Germany's policy, politically and financially; treats of her internal political situation; of German influence in her military organization; of the eleventh-hour trifling of the Porte with Great Britain in respect to the German warships, the Goeben and the Breslau; of the increasing German influence in her military counsels; of the abolition of the "Capitulations," Great Britain's temperate complaint of her hostile acts; and finally of Turkey's certain enmity to the Entente powers, the withdrawal of their ambassadors and Turkey's proclamation of a holy war against Great Britain, France and Russia.

The course of events leading to Italy's participation in the war is outlined; her mistrust of Austria's policy toward Serbia; her demand for compensating concessions for Austria's gains in the Balkans; the influence of her domestic politics and the force of the national spirit; her occupation of Valona; the efforts of Germany to secure appeasement of Italian demands; and her denunciation of the Triple Alliance and association with the Entente powers.

In his concluding chapter the author estimates some of the forces of nationality operating in the European conflict; rapidly reviews the influence of the commercial rivalry between Germany and Great Britain; the unrest and dissatisfaction in Germany owing to her relative geographic inferiority to Great Britain and France; finds Germany's ambitious Weltpolitik not unreasonable in principle; shows the increase in her navy to have been disproportionate to her political and commercial needs compared with that of Great Britain and to have roused Great Britain's alarm and caused her naval augmentation; contends that the Balkan question, as involved in Germany's eastern ambitions, emphasized the rivalry of Teuton and Slav and was the great question that pressed Germany to war.

The bulk of the material the author has presented will be looked for vainly in the pages of ephemeral publications when the convulsive actions that are now shocking the world are spent and the new world relations are to be shaped, and when the American public should not be silent as to the part its government may take in such shaping and in the future relations our country may establish with the belligerents of to-day.

The causes of such a world calamity are of intensest interest to Americans. The subject is pregnant with lessons for us as individual citizens, politically, commercially and socially. War determines no superiority save that of physical power and demoniacal strategy, the basest and most destructive of the instruments of human perversity.

The book, in its outward form and in typography and illustration, is handsome. The illustrations are numerous and excellently chosen to supplement the text both pictorially and instructively. There are, besides, a useful chronological table and an extended practical index.

THE MENORAH CONVENTION.

Delegates From All Sections of the United States.

The fourth annual Menorah Convention, held here during the week of December 27, proved to be the most enthusiastic and most representative gathering in the history of the Menorah movement. Delegates and members were present from Eastern, Middle Western and Far Western universities, including Minnesota, Omaha, Wisconsin, California and Washington (Seattle). The women's colleges (Hunter and Radcliffe) sent large delegations, and one co-educational university (Cal.) sent a woman to represent it.

The sessions convened on Monday morning, December 27, in the rooms of the Philomathean Society, College Hall. After presentation of credentials and seating of delegates and deputies, applications of new societies for admission into the Intercollegiate Association were considered. Five societies were admitted, four admitted conditionally and nine rejected for failure to fulfill requirements.

After an informal luncheon served in College Hall, the Chancellor presented his report, giving a survey of the Menorah activities which touched upon the growth of the Menorah movement since its inception in 1906; the Menorah College of Lecturers; the Menorah prizes; the Menorah libraries; the Menorah courses of study and syllabi; the Menorah Journal; the Menorah classes; the Graduate Phase of the Movement and the relations of the Menorah with other organizations.

He showed that the growth of the movement had far exceeded the fondest hopes of its founders, and that its total membership, now about 3,500, was still but a fraction of what it would be in the course of a few years. With the admission of the new societies and the success that was attending the present stages of about a dozen other Menorah societies, the Intercollegiate would feel itself on a firm foundation with more than fifty constituent societies affiliated with it.

At a formal reception given Monday evening by Philadelphia Alumni, the delegates were welcomed by Dr. Solomon Solis-Cohen, president of the Philadelphia "Kehilla." He said in part:

"The Jews have the right to exist everywhere. There is no need for the Jew to apologize for either his life, his existence or his career, religion or manner of living. Don't whine and don't apologize, but brace up and go ahead as you have the right to do. There has been some censure of the Jew from people of our own race who mourn the absence of a Spinoza, a D'Israeli, a Heine, among our people today. What of it? We have as much right now to be independent without a Spinoza or a D'Israeli or Heine as in the days when these giants lived. All that the Jews need remember is to cease whining, stop apologizing and go right ahead."

Professor I. Leo Sharfman, of Michigan, president of the Intercollegiate Menorah Association, in responding, expressed the thanks of the Association for the cordial reception and the interest evidenced by the community in the purposes for which the Menorah stands. He lamented the fact that due recognition is not given in American universities to those who devote themselves to the larger cultural activities and moral problems presented, and he asked for the encouragement of alumni to those giving up, at a great sacrifice, time and effort to such considerations. College graduates appealed to interest themselves in Menorah work and the ideals that are nurtured and upheld by the movement.

The day sessions on Tuesday, Wednesday and Thursday were devoted to the consideration of the officers' reports, the reports of delegates, problems of administration, the adoption of certain recommendations, including a change of policy toward the admission of new societies and new members, the future of the Menorah Journal and the election of officers.

Among those considered and approved was the imposing of a per capita tax upon the constituent societies to help support the Intercollegiate Association. It was decided, also, to hold each society responsible for the subscription to the Menorah Journal of each of its members. In connection with the Journal it was stated that public approval had been instantaneous and hearty. The Journal was maintaining a high standard and providing both intellectual nourishment and spiritual reinforcement.

The Menorah's interest in Jewish scholarship was shown in the session at the Dropsie College on Tuesday evening, devoted to papers by leading Jewish scholars, including Professor Julian Morgenstern of the Hebrew Union College, Professor Israel Friedlaender of the Jewish Theological Seminary, and Professor Max Margolis of the Dropsie College.

Dr. Cyrus Adler, '81, president of the Dropsie College, in a short memorial paid tribute to the memory of Professor Solomon Schlechter.

The Annual Convention Dinner, held Wednesday evening at the Hotel Adelphia, will go down in Menorah history as a memorable occasion. Stimulating after-dinner speeches were made by Dr. Solomon Solis-Cohen, Dr. Cyrus Adler, Dr. H. M. Kallen, Mr. Samuel Strauss, Judge Mayer Sulzberger, and others.

Judge Sulzberger said in part: "I do not trouble myself about the definitions of Jew or Judaism. These definitions are mere words used by eloquent speakers and deep thinkers, but mean very little to the great world outside. The Jew is one and indivisible. He is a fact, not a theory or a definition. The most important thing that the Menorah should do is to build Jewish character. Learning is only of value if it arouses character by broadening the vision and deepening the intellect. Our schools and colleges are full of young ·men and young women who will never be of any importance to the world because they have not converted their learning into character."

As a mark of respect to the gallant Jewish students of European universities who have lost their lives in the war abroad, all assembled rose while a short eulogy was offered.

Following the custom of alternating between the East and the West, the convention next year will be held at the University of Minnesota.

Botanical Society of Pennsylvania.

The next meeting of the Botanical Society of Pennsylvania will be held in Botanical Hall on Friday evening, January 21, at 8 o'clock. The program includes, "A Review of Current Botanical Literature," by Miss Martha M. Hollinshead; "Studies of the Fruit," by Mr. D. W. Steckbeck; "Notes on the Pan-American Exposition," by Miss Lois M. Otis.

OLD PENN

HOUSTON HALL, WEST PHILADELPHIA.

Published every Saturday during the Academic Year of the University of Pennsylvania.

Publishers, UNIVERSITY OF PENNSYLVANIA.

Edited by George E. Nitzsche and Members of the University Staff.

SUBSCRIPTION.............................$2.00 PER YEAR
PAYABLE IN ADVANCE.

Single copies, ten cents.
Postage free to all countries in Postal Union.

Checks, drafts and orders should be made payable to OLD PENN

All correspondence should be addressed
OLD PENN, Houston Hall,
University of Pennsylvania,
Philadelphia, Pa.
Telephones { Bell, Baring 100.
{ Keystone, West 42-79A.

Entered as second-class matter October 17, 1903, at the post office at Philadelphia, Pa., under Act of March 3, 1879.

This magazine is devoted to the general public work of the University,—local and national, and to its work in other lands, as well as to the interests of its great body of alumni.

PHILADELPHIA, JANUARY 15, 1916.

A VALUABLE GIFT TO THE LIBRARY.

The Library of the University of Pennsylvania has been presented with a copy of a University of Louvain publication which has just been printed in Paris. It consists of a volume of lectures given at the College of France by Paul Delannoy, Professor and Librarian of the University of Louvain. This volume is of particular interest to the University because it has had the benefit during the past year of the instruction given by Professor Albert Joseph Carnoy, who was appointed Research Professor of Greek at the University after the destruction of the University of Louvain, of which faculty Dr. Carnoy was a member. Driven from it with colleagues and students by the ruthless destruction of its buildings by the German invaders of Belgium, he (with his wife) is a constant appeal for sympathy and help for the people of Belgium.

Founded in 1422, the University opened in 1432 with five faculties—Theology, Arts, Medicine, Canonical and Civil Law. Louvain, like Philadelphia to-day, was a great industrial center, and its prosperous manufacturers and merchants and the Government gave it at all times substantial support. Ravaged by succeeding invasions, their great wealth of industry was scattered in distant countries, but in spite of foreign and civil wars the University flourished until the Germans put the torch to its venerable buildings

534

and its great library and its collection of precious historical portraits and manuscripts and documents relating to the long and honorable growth of the University. Like our own University Louvain was the victim at times of civil disturbance, but foreign invasion inflicted the last and most severe blow. The College of Philadelphia lost its Charter and its property in the period of political unrest that followed the War of Independence, but with the union of the restored College and its rival, the University of the State of Pennsylvania, the growth of the University has been steady and prosperous. Louvain has reason to be proud of its long roll of illustrious men—Erasmus, Lipsius, Vesali, and many others who figure in Prof. Delannoy's story of its history. Even under Napoleon its existence was suspended, its schools transferred to Brussels, its Library to Paris, but it shared in the benefit of the independence of Belgium, and grew with its growth. Its splendid Library building, destroyed by the German conquerors, was one of the great glories of Louvain. Really founded in 1634, it gathered there the scattered treasures of its old Colleges. Prof. Delannoy, as Librarian, speaks enthusiastically of its uses, saying that already in the Middle Ages a proverb was current that "A Convent without a Library was like a Fort without a Magazine," and quoting Thomas à Kempis, who said: "It is like a table without food, a garden without flowers, or a purse without money." Louvain had a large collection of manuscripts from the Ninth to the Seventeenth Century, many rare incunabula, and nearly 300,000 books, besides a wealth of University Archives. The Austrian and the French invasion scattered many of its treasures, but most of them were recovered later on; but the Germans, in spite of their pride of culture, put the torch to them. Louvain, however, looks forward to its restoration with peace, as an evidence of the triumph of right over force, of civilization over barbarism, and will again inscribe on its new Library that which stood on its old doors, "Sapientia aedificavit sibi domum"—words that might well be used by our own University.—J. G. Rosengarten.

FRANKLIN'S BIRTHDAY TO BE CELEBRATED.

Franklin's birthday, Monday, January 17, will be celebrated by many schools and institutions throughout the United States. At the University of Pennsylvania Hon. Hampon L. Carson will deliver an illustrated talk on the founder of the University. The talk will be given at four o'clock in the auditorium of the Houston Club, and will be open to the public. At noon of Franklin's birthday the members of the Poor Richard Club of Philadelphia will place a wreath on the grave of the philosopher. They will proceed, headed by a band, from their quaint little club house at 239 South Camac Street, to the famous old Quaker Cemetery, and with a few simple ceremonies place a floral tribute on the grave of the great statesman. The Poor Richard Club is also asking the various public schools to observe the day by starting the morning sessions with a brief talk on the life and achievements of Franklin, or by reading paragraphs from his writings. The club has also sent the following memorial to each school house in the city, to be read to the pupils on the morning of Franklin's birthday:

BENJAMIN FRANKLIN.
Born, Boston, Mass., January 17, 1706.
Died, Philadelphia, April 17, 1790.

Let us pause, for a brief time, on this anniversary day, to pay homage to the memory of Benjamin Franklin, printer, editor, author, founder of the University of Pennsylvania and of the Philadelphia Library, philosopher, scientist, statesman, diplomatist.

His name is carved in granite and bronze; his homely quips, quaint counsel and profound wisdom are quoted oft in the tongues of twenty nations. His genius for research opened the door to illimitable accomplishment for those who follow him. His gentleness, his benevolence, his beautiful devotion to kindred and country have endeared him to all mankind. Bound to no sect, yet respecting all, and respected by all. If he had a fault common to his times, he had virtues uncommon to all times. His spirit lives; the passing of centuries shall not dim the luster of his fame; his memory shall be cherished to the end of days. A self-made man, a scholar among the learned, the peer of peers, honored by the highest—yet ever simply, B. Franklin, Printer. A truly great man, in mind, heart and soul.

So distinguished and many-sided were his talents that his influence on the minds of men has been greater than that of any other American.

Poor Richard Club, Philadelphia.
January 17, 1916.

Greek Art from China.

The University Museum has purchased two pieces of ancient Chinese sculpture which it considers not only among its finest treasures but in many respects the most remarkable additions to modern collections of Chinese sculpture, of which there is very little outside of China. Recently China forbade sending out any more ancient art treasures and it is doubtful if the Western world ever will get any more statues equal to those just acquired. These were shipped out during the revolution and not a great deal is known of them. They are less than life size and came from one of the buried cities of Turkestan, cities once prosperous, but now wholly covered by sand. The dry sand has kept the statues in a marvelous state of preservation. They are of marble and originally were colored, with green, gold, blue and red, traces of which can still be seen. One has a peculiar headdress and is supposed to be Kwan-yin, the goddess of mercy. The other has a plain headdress and its character is unknown.

These statues date from the Fifth Century at about the time when Chinese sculpture was in its flower. The astonishing thing is that the work shows plainly Greek inspiration. It is wholly free from that convention which later Chinese art shows and it is presumed that the sculptor was influenced by the wave of Greek influence in art which followed the triumphs of Alexander in the East. The execution is admirable and the fine handling of the drapery is characteristic of Greek art at its best. Until these statues were found it was not supposed that Chinese art was affected by Greek influence. These will be placed on exhibition at the forthcoming Exhibition of Oriental Art.

So rare are Chinese sculptures that they are sought by all museums. At the outbreak of the war a Paris dealer, who had offered some sculptures from China to the Louvre, found no market there and they were shipped to the University Museum on approval. Before the Museum had made arrangements for their purchase word was received from the Louvre that they had purchased them and asked that they be returned to Paris. This is considered an interesting sidelight on the war.

Pan-American Delegates Visit University.

Representing practically every Latin-American country, 125 delegates of the Second Pan-American Scientific Congress, which closed last Saturday in Washington, visited the University of Pennsylvania on Tuesday morning, January 11. In Houston Hall the delegates were formally received and welcomed on behalf of the University by Provost Edgar F. Smith. Brief addresses were delivered by the Provost and by Honorable John Barrett, who was in charge of the party. These addresses were responded to by several of the delegates. A committee consisting of a few officials and eighty-three students at the University from Latin-American countries, conducted the visitors about the campus and various buildings of the University. The delegates were grouped according to the departments of the University in which they were most interested, and each of these groups was conducted by a Latin-American student guide. Honorable John Barrett, the Director General of the Pan-American Union, was in charge of the party during their stay in Philadelphia. He was assisted by Boaz W. Long, U. S. Minister to Salvador; Maddin Summers, U. S. Consul at Sao Paulo, Brazil, and Stedman S. Hanks, of the Department of State.

The delegates, according to Mr. Barrett, were made up of some of the most celebrated citizens of the Latin-American countries. Among these was General F. D. Legitime, at one time President of Haiti; Dr. Juan B. Ambrosetti, head of the Buenos Aires Museum; Rear Admiral Juan A. Martin, the reorganizer of the Argentine Navy; Dr. Vital Brazil, of Brazil, said to be one of the leading authorities on snake bites; Dr. Manuel de Oliveira Lima, who was invited to accept a chair at Harvard University as a lecturer on international law; Dr. Luis Anderson, of Costa Rica, another authority on international law, and other men of similar standing.

Episcopal Students Entertained.

About 150 Episcopal Church students were entertained at a banquet at the Roosevelt Monday evening, January 10, and listened to addresses by Bishop Rhinelander, Rev. G. A. Johnston Ross, of New York; Mr. Franklin Spencer Edmonds, '03 L., and Rev. John R. Hart, Jr. These Church banquets, which are held each year by several of the different communions, are now an established feature of the year's work

NATIONAL COLLEGIATE ATHLETIC ASSOCIATION.

Tenth Annual Convention in New York City.

One hundred and fifty delegates took part in the tenth annual convention of the National Collegiate Athletic Association at the Hotel Astor, New York, on December 28. In addition to the discussion on athletics, reports were read on football and other sports, with recommendations for the betterment of college athletics and a clearer definition of the rules governing the same.

A plea for a system of collegiate athletics in which every student would have a chance to participate was made by Dr. Harry A. Garfield, president of Williams College.

Dean Howard McClenahan, of Princeton University, spoke on athletic standards, and approved of the faculty controlling all athletic activities in the colleges.

Professor Albert Le Fevre, of the University of Virginia, speaking on schedule making and institutional responsibility, declared against itinerant coaches and the playing of games with other institutions playing ineligibles.

Professor Robert N. Corwin, of Yale, spoke on college ideals and athletics, and in conclusion said he believed that athletics should become an important feature of university education, and that they should, therefore, be more closely associated with the intra-curricular aims.

The following officers of the organization and committees were elected: . President, Le Baron Briggs, Harvard; vice-president, James R. Angell, Chicago University; secretary-treasurer, Frank W. Nicolson, Wesleyan University.

Executive Committee—First District, Professor R. N. Corwin, Yale; second district, Professor Joseph E. Raycroft, Princeton; third district, Professor C. H. Herty, University of North Carolina; fourth district, H. E. Buchanan, Tennessee; fifth district, Professor G. A. Goodenough, Illinois; sixth district, Professor C. L. Brewer, Missouri; seventh district, Professor D. G. Owen, Oklahoma; eighth district, Professor E. J. Stewart, Oregon Agricultural College.

RULES COMMITTEE.

Football—Dr. H. L. Williams, University of Minnesota, chairman; E. K. Hall, Dartmouth; Dr. J. A. Babbitt, Haverford; Lieutenant Phil Hayes, United States Military Academy; Professor W. C. Savage, Oberlin; Professor S. C. Williams, Iowa State; Professor W. A. Lambeth, University of Virginia, and representatives of Harvard, Yale, Princeton, Pennsylvania, Cornell, Annapolis and Chicago.

Track Athletics—Frank Castleman, Ohio State University, chairman; Dr. J. L. Griffith, Drake University, and Romayn Berry, Columbia.

Basket-ball—Dr. J. E. Raycroft, Princeton, chairman; Dr. James Naismith, University of Kansas; Ralph Morgan, University of Pennsylvania; Oswald Tower, Andover; Dr. L. J. Cooke, University of Minnesota; Director L. W. St. John, Ohio State; Director Lory Prentiss, Lawrenceville School; J. F. Bohler, Washington College, and H. F. Sturdee, St. John's College.

Association (Soccer) Football—Dr. J. A. Babbitt, Haverford, chairman; W. F. Garcelon, Bates; Dr. P. S. Page, Phillips-Andover; Dr. George W. Orton, University of Pennsylvania; C. H. Mapes, Columbia University; Professor C. L. Brewer, University of Missouri, and A. S. Dyment, University of Oregon.

CHRISTIAN ASSOCIATION NOTES.

Dr. John Douglas Adam, of Hartford Seminary, who comes to the University to-day to spend a week speaking at the daily Chapel services and in the churches on two Sundays, is a noted scholar and orator. He comes under the new plan instituted in December, whereby during one week in each month a prominent national Church leader visits the University and addresses the students on the fundamental questions of religion. Dr. Adam will devote his afternoons to interviews and will take a number of his meals in the different Fraternity Houses, so that he will come into personal contact with a considerable number of students. On Monday evening, January 17, he will speak at the annual Presbyterian students' banquet, at the Roosevelt. Plans are under way for a meeting with members of the Faculty on Sunday afternoon, January 23.

An interesting journey through Japan and the war stricken province of Shantung, China, was enjoyed by William H. Adolph, '12 C., '15 Ph.D., who has just gone to China as a missionary. Dr. Adolph is to provide training in chemistry for the large number of young men who are availing themselves increasingly of the educational opportunities provided by Shantung Christian University, Tsinan-fu, Shantung, China, where he may be addressed. Dr. Adolph writes: "We had an extremely pleasant voyage and did not get seasick. I left San Francisco October 2 and arrived in Tsingtao October 30, having transshipped at Kobe, Japan. It is eight hours by rail from Tsingtao to Tsinan-fu.

"The country out here is flat—just a few big hills here and there, but the rest is as smooth as a drawing board, and when the river overflows it naturally overflows it all at once. Tsinan-fu is an interesting city, thoroughly Chinese inside its thirty-foot wall, with a modern German and European quarter to the West. The Japanese have military patrols at stations and bridges, have renamed the stations with Japanese names, and replaced the Chinese railroad officials and employes by Japanese. Not a Chinese has been allowed to keep his job. Two thousand Germans were deported from Tsinan-fu and fifteen thousand Japs imported.

"At Tsinan-fu building operations are now in progress. The medical department of the university is well equipped and has one of the finest hospitals and dispensaries in the far East. The College Department, the Theological Department and the Teachers' College are moving to the new Campus, which will be fine when finished. They are building the new Chemistry laboratory, and I shall have much of the equipping of that building in my hands.

"Dr. J. B. Neal, '83 M., is Dean of the Medical College, and Dr. W. M. Schultz, '05 M., is one of the faculty. The latter will return to Philadelphia within the next few months. The staff of the College consists of twelve Americans and Europeans and about twenty Chinese professors and assistants. The College was founded just fifty years ago. I am living in a corner of the old College compound and am studying the Chinese language at the rate of five hours per day."

BASKET-BALL.

Cornell, 17; Pennsylvania, 19.

Pennsylvania won from Cornell in basket-ball at Weightman Hall in an intercollegiate game on December 8, by the score of 19 to 17. It was a hard-earned victory and the score at the end of the regular periods was 17 to 17, necessitating an extra five-minute period, in which Jefford made the winning field goal. The line-up:

PENNSYLVANIA.

	—Goals—			
	Field.	Foul.	Assts.	Pts.
Martin, forward	1	0	0	2
Williamson, forward	0	0	2	0
Jefford, center	3	0	0	6
McNichol, guard	3	3	1	9
Jones, guard	1	0	2	2
Totals	8	3	5	19

CORNELL.

	—Goals—			
	Field.	Foul.	Assts.	Pts.
Lunden, forward	3	0	2	6
Brown, forward	2	2	0	6
Sutterby, center	0	0	1	0
Shelton, guard	1	0	0	2
Ashmeade, guard	0	3	0	3
Totals	6	5	3	17

Fouls committed, Pennsylvania 14, Cornell 7. Time of halves, twenty minutes. Referee, Tom Thorpe, Columbia. Umpire, W. Lush, New York University. Score at half-time, Pennsylvania 11, Cornell 10.

FOOTBALL.

Robert Folwell Football Coach.

After a long period of discussion and consideration, Robert Folwell was elected coach of the 1916 football team, on January 4. The selection is one that has been received with great satisfaction both by graduates and undergraduates.

Folwell was captain of the 1907 team, and, like Torrey and Hollenback, who were his teammates, was an All-American man. He came to Pennsylvania from the Haverford School. At Pennsylvania he became famous not only in football, but in track athletics and wrestling. He was one of the few athletes to win his Varsity letter in three sports in a single year. He played in the backfield on the famous 1904 and 1905 elevens, and was the backbone of the team's secondary defence.

Folwell's college coaching has been confined to three institutions, Lafayette, Johns Hopkins and Washington and Jefferson. While at Lafayette his team beat both Princeton and Cornell. His most conspicuous success has been achieved at Washington and Jefferson. With only three or four hundred students to draw from he has turned out teams which beat Yale twice in succession. He has shown wonderful skill in developing new material, for, in spite of losing nearly all of last year's team by graduation, he turned out an eleven this fall which lost but a single team, that to Pittsburgh.

A Voluntary Course in Military Instruction.

A voluntary course in military instruction at the University of Pennsylvania will soon become a reality, if the plans formulated by a number of representative students at a meeting held on January 6, are carried out.

The chief features of this course, when it is established at the University, will be that:—

(1) It will be entirely voluntary.

(2) It will take 84 hours a year, or about three hours a week.

(3) It will be under the supervision of an officer detailed by the War Department, who will be a member of the faculty.

(4) It will be an intensive course, designed to train men to be officers in case of need, with as little time as possible spent on the mere mechanical details of close-order drill.

(5) If approved by the faculty, it is to be counted as credit toward a degree, probably as an equivalent to gymnasium.

Negotiations with the United States War Department at Washington, carried on by Captain J. Franklin McFadden, have reached such a point that now it is only necessary for the authorities of the University to take action, backed by the approval of the student body, for the course to be established at the University.

The movement has the support of a large majority of undergraduates, and of many prominent alumni, chief among them being Secretary of War Garrison and William A. Redding, president of the General Alumni Society, both of whom have assisted materially in the preliminary stages of the movement.

A Commission to Study Grippe.

An intensive study of the question of pneumonia will be made by a commission appointed January 11, by Director Wilmer Krusen, ex-'93 M., of the Department of Health and Charities. The recent epidemic of grip and pneumonia occasioned the appointment of a commission.

Director Krusen appointed the members from those eminent either for clinical work or for their ability as laboratory research workers. The city laboratories will be placed at their disposal. Dr. David Riesman, '92 M., professor of clinical medicine in the University of Pennsylvania and the Philadelphia Polyclinic, will be chairman. Other members are:

Dr. Hobart A. Hare, '84 M., professor of therapeutics at Jefferson Medical College.

Dr. Judson Daland, '82 M., professor of clinical medicine in the Medico-Chirurgical College.

Dr. William Egbert Robertson, '92 M., professor of the practice of medicine, Temple University.

Dr. Randle C. Rosenberger (Jeff.), professor of hygiene and bacteriology in the Jefferson Medical College and the Women's Medical College.

Dr. Paul A. Lewis, director of the Ayer Clinical Laboratory of the Pennsylvania Hospital and director of the pathological department of the Henry Phipps Institute.

Dr. John A. Kolmer, '08 M., professor of pathology, Philadelphia Polyclinic; instructor of experimental pathology at the University of Pennsylvania.

AMONG THE ALUMNI.

The firm of Wessel and Aarons has been dissolved consequent to the election of Henry N. Wessel, '91 L., as Judge of Common Pleas Court, No. 2, of the County of Philadelphia. Alfred Aarons, '02 L., will continue the practice of law at the offices heretofore occupied by the firm in the Penn Square Building.

Dr. and Mrs. Herbert M. Howe, of 1622 Locust Street, have announced the engagement of their daughter, Miss Edith Howe, to Dr. Halsey De Wolf, of Providence, R. I. Dr. De Wolf is the son of Winthrop De Wolf, a descendant of Governor Winthrop, of Massachusetts. He was graduated from Harvard in 1892, and from the University of Pennsylvania Medical School in 1897. He is practicing in Providence, R. I.

The annual dinner of the New England Alumni will be held at the Boston City Club on Saturday evening, January 22. The principal speaker and guest of honor will be Josiah H. Penniman, LL.D., Vice-Provost of the University. The officers of the society are: President, James C. Irwin, '90 C.; vice-president, Henry H. Patterson, '11 D.; secretary-treasurer, Harvey C. Dever, '08 C. The Executive Committee includes the officers above mentioned and R. H. Cope, '08 C., and F. C. Farquhar, '00 C.

John Dennis Mahoney, '01 C., Professor of English in West Philadelphia High School, delivered a lecture on physical culture before the students of the West Philadelphia at West Branch Y. M. C. A., on Saturday evening, January 8, in which he denounced cigarette smoking, and drew a line between indulgences which are harmful only from over-indulgence and those which are essentially vicious.

R. Robinson Barrett, assistant chief of the Division of Housing and Sanitation of the Department of Public Health, resigned to accept a position with a New York corporation. Mr. Barrett, who is a civil engineer, is said by his associates to be one of the most popular men in the Health Department. He graduated from the University of Pennsylvania in 1907, when he was first honor man. He was president of his class for four years, and a member of the Varsity four and eight oar rowing crews. Mr. Barrett is also a graduate of the Wenonah Military Academy of New Jersey, and is president of the Alumni Association of that school.

Rudolph Sze, '14 C., the captain of the chess team and a remarkable player of 1912 and 1913, has written an interesting letter to J. V. Magee, Jr., '87 C., from Tangshan Engineering College, Tangshan, North China, under date of December 6. Mr. Sze will join the "Good Companion Chess Problem Club," but declines the honor of being foreign vice-president, as there are few chess players in China, who are in the problem solving class.

Charles A. Coulomb, Ph.D., 1910, has been appointed district superintendent by the Committee on Elementary Schools of the Board of Education. Dr. Coulomb was supervising principal of Glenwood School and a teacher of pedagogy at Temple University evening classes.

Dr. Thomas S. Roberts, '85 M., of Minneapolis, Minn., retired from the general practice of medicine on January 1, to secure additional time to devote to the ornithological work of the Department of Animal Biology, and the Zoological Museum, and field work of the State Natural History Survey at the University of Minnesota.

Dr. Walter Chrystie, '83 M., of Bryn Mawr, has been elected president of the new Main Line Branch of the Montgomery Medical Society, with temporary quarters at the Merion Cricket Club, at Haverford, where meetings will be held twice a month. The first regular meeting for scientific discussion was held on Monday night, with Dr. Hobart A. Hare and Dr. Thomas McCrea, of Philadelphia, as the speakers.

Leon L. Strohecker, '14 Sp. Arch., and Miss Helen M. Hoover, both of Reading, Pa., were married in New York City on December 24. Mr. Strohecker is a graduate of Reading High School and is engaged in the practice of architecture in New York.

Dr. William J. Fuchs, '06 D., 199 Gates Avenue, Brooklyn, N. Y., announced under date of January 10: "Two future sons of Pennsylvania arrived in town safe and sound on January 6, 1916, to Dr. and Mrs. William J. Fuchs. Mother and babes doing well."

Dr. Lloyd C. Robinson, '13 D., of Morrisville, Vt., announces the arrival of John Daniels Robinson, another son of Pennsylvania.

Graham Starr Made Assistant Examiner of Civil Service Commission.

Graham Starr, '13 Arts, was suggested by Dean Arthur Hobson Quinn, of the College, in reply to a request from the Chief Examiner for a position as assistant for the Civil Service Commission. Dean Quinn has received the following letter from Mr. Starr:

"This letter is another word of thanks for your kindness in proposing me for the position of Assistant Examiner for the Civil Service Commission. A few days ago the commission published the results of the examination held to determine who should be the permanent appointee to the vacancy. About twenty men and women tried for the position and of that number three secured a passing grade or better. I was fortunate enough to lead that trio with an average of 76.8 and was immediately given the position as a permanent proposition. Mr. Peter Bolger, secretary of the commission, suggested this morning that you, as the proposer of my name, would be interested in the outcome of the examination."

Mr. Starr is a graduate of Central High School and a member of the Zelosophic Society.

A Western Branch of the Japanese Alumni Society.

Mr. Tsunezo Meiji, a professor in the Osako Higher Commercial School, one of our best students, who specialized in transportation and other business courses, has carried with him the spirit of Pennsylvania into Western Japan, as is shown in a letter to Prof. Emory R. Johnson, under date of December 9, from which we have the pleasure of quoting the following paragraphs:

"Many thanks for your kind letter informing me of the arrival of Mr. Oda, who had been so kindly received by you through my introduction. Simultaneously with your letter I received one from Mr. Oda, telling that he has become so much interested in his studies in the University.

"As for me, everything is going on quite well, and in the school I am giving to students lectures on accounting, railway transportation and business mathematics (seven hours a week), and have a mind to write a book on the principles of accounting in the coming year."

"There are just ten alumni and ex-students of the University of Pennsylvania in Osaka, Kyoto and Kobe. They have established the Western Branch of the University of Pennsylvania Alumni Association of Japan, and are holding meetings twice a year. Mr. Masao Matsukata, the president of the Naniwa Bank (Osaka); Mr. Jiro Itami, the manager of the Kobe Branch of the Nippon Yusen Kaisha (Japan Mail S. S. Co.); Dr. Tesshi Kono, the director of the Kono Hospital; Dr. Rojuki Ogata, the director of the Osaka Dental School, and Dr. Riichiro Sayeki, the director of the Sayeki Hospital, Kyoto, are the leading members."

NOTES AND COMMENTS.

Dr. A. A. Goldenweiser, of the Department of Anthropology, Columbia University, New York, conducted a discussion at the last meeting of the Anthropological Discussion Group, which took place in Room 307, College Hall, at 4 P. M., Monday, January 10. Dr. Goldenweiser is an authority on the subject of primitive social organization, and the subject of the discussion was in this field.

All men who have won places on the University debate team will be eligible for the Frazier Prize Debate, to be held Wednesday evening, January 19, in Price Hall of the Law School. Prizes of $75 and $25 will be awarded to the speakers who win first and second places. The subject of the Frazier Debate is "Armament," whether or not an increase in our army and navy is demanded by our best interests.

Professor Carl Kelsey, of the Wharton School of Finance and Commerce, was the principal speaker at the Charity Exhibit in the Widener Building, on January 8, and said in part: "I have had the opportunity of studying the work of charitable organizations, and I have never found a man or woman of wealth supporting them for a selfish or unworthy motive. It is true, the organizations here sustain a co-operative relationship, but their functions are different, and each has its particular work and problems."

While attending the sessions of the Pan-American Scientific Congress at Washington, Professor Herman V. Ames, Dean of the Graduate School, was a guest of the Brown University Alumni Association of Maryland and the District of Columbia at a luncheon at the University Club.

"Rameses' Goat," a scenario, written by C. E. Summer, '18 Arch., and N. W. Corey, '18 Arch., was selected by the Architectural Society for their annual play. The play will be given the latter part of February, in a place to be selected.

The concert of the Musical Clubs, which was to have been given at Haddonfield, N. J., on January 7, has been postponed to February 7.

The first Ford ambulance of the twenty that John McFadden, Jr., has come over here to get has been given to him. It was quite the proper thing that this should be the gift of the French War Relief Committee of the Emergency Aid, and at the weekly meeting of the committee on January 5, the gift was unanimously voted.

ADVANCE ANNOUNCEMENTS.

(Period Ending) SUNDAY, JANUARY 23, 1916.

SUNDAY, JANUARY 16.

11.00 A. M. University Service. Professor John Douglas Adam, D.D., of Hartford Seminary. Central Congregational Church.*
2.00-6.00 P. M. The University Museum. Open to Visitors. Thirty-third and Spruce Streets.*
3.00 P. M. Hospital Vesper Service. University Hospital.*
6.00-9.00 P. M. University Settlement. Open to Visitors. Twenty-sixth and Lombard Streets.*
8.00 P. M. Professor John Douglas Adam. Tabernacle Presbyterian Church.*

MONDAY, JANUARY 17.
FRANKLIN'S BIRTHDAY.

12.30 P. M. Freshman Chapel Service. Rev. John Douglas Adam, D.D. Weightman Hall.*
1.00 P. M. Dental Chapel Service. Dental Building.*
4.00 P. M. Address. "A Talk on Benjamin Franklin," by the Hon. Hampton L. Carson. Auditorium, Houston Hall.*

TUESDAY, JANUARY 18.

12.30 P. M. Sophomore Chapel Service. Rev. John Douglas Adam, D.D. Houston Hall.*
4.00 P. M. Free Public Lecture. "The Religion of Ancient Persia—The Idea of God," by Professor Albert J. Carnoy, Late of the University of Louvain. Auditorium, Houston Hall.*
8.00 P. M. Musical Clubs Concert. Bethlehem Presbyterian Church.***
8.00 P. M. Basket-ball. Yale vs. Pennsylvania. New Haven.***

WEDNESDAY, JANUARY 19.

12.30 P. M. Junior Chapel Service. Rev. John Douglas Adam, D.D. Houston Hall.*
2.30 P. M. Museum Lecture for Teachers and Members. "Ruined Cities in Peten, Guatemala." Illustrated. Mr. Herbert J. Spinden. University Museum.*
5.00 P. M. Address, Internationalism and Pacificism, by Wm. English Walling, under the auspices of the Intercollegiate Society for the Discussion of Socialism. Houston Hall.**
8.00 P. M. Free Public Lecture. "The Religious Question in the Philippines," by the Rev. John P. Chidwick, D.D., Auspices of the Catholic Students' Organization Committee. Auditorium, Houston Hall.*
8.00 P. M. Frazier Prize Debate. "Armament." The Public is Invited. Price Hall, Law School.*

THURSDAY, JANUARY 20.

12.30 P. M. Senior Chapel Service. Rev. John Douglas Adam, D.D. Houston Hall.*
4.00 P. M. Free Public Lecture in French. "Flaubert." Professor Pierre F. Geroud. Houston Hall.*
7.00-10.00 P. M. Flower Astronomical Observatory.

Open to Visitors. On West Chester or Ardmore Trolley, one mile from Sixty-ninth Street Terminal.*
8.00 P. M. British Society. Illustrated Lecture. "Experience with the American Ambulance Corps at Paris." Mr. Reuben Lenzer. Houston Hall.**

FRIDAY, JANUARY 21.

12.00 M. All Undergradutes' Chapel Service. Rev. John Douglas Adam, D.D. Weightman Hall, Gymnasium.**
8.00 P. M. Botanical Society of Pennsylvania Program: "A Review of Current Botanical Literature," by Miss Martha H. Hollinshead; "Studies of Fruit," Dr. D. W. Steckbeck; "Notes on the Pan-American Exposition," by Miss Lois M. Otis. Botanical Hall.*
8.00 P. M. Musical Clubs Concert. Philadelphia Girls' Normal School.***
8.30 P. M. Rush Society Lecture. Dr. F. M. Allen of the Rockefeller Institute of Medical Research. College of Physicians.**

SATURDAY, JANUARY 22.

9.30 A. M. Botanical Excursion to Crum Creek and Ridley Creek. Leave at 9.30 A. M., by Media Short Line, from Sixty-ninth Street Station.
3.00 P. M. Free Public Lecture. "The Sea and the Sailor in Fiction." Professor Edward C. Wesselhoeft. Houston Hall Auditorium.*
3.30 P. M. Free Public Lecture. "A Naturalist in Central Africa." Illustrated. Mr. James Chapin. University Museum.*
8.00 P. M. Basket-ball. Dartmouth vs. Pennsylvania. Gymnasium.***
8.00 P. M. Musical Clubs Concert. University Extension Society. Witherspoon Hall.***

SUNDAY, JANUARY 23.

11.00 A. M. University Service. Rev. John Douglas Adam. Tabernacle Presbyterian Church. Chestnut and Thirty-seventh Streets.*
2.00-6.00 P. M. The University Museum. Open to Visitors. Thirty-third and Spruce Streets.*
3.00 P. M. Hospital Vesper Service. University Hospital.*
6.00-9.00 P. M. University Settlement. Open to Visitors. Twenty-sixth and Lombard Streets.*

Note.—*Open to the public. **Open to Students and Members of the Faculty and Special Guests. ***Admission by Card or Ticket.

Printing for Educators

EDUCATORS are not supposed to familiarize themselves with the mechanical details of a printing plant. It would be better in some cases if they did so. For example, if every teacher knew the advantages of having his pamphlets and books set by the wonderful MONOTYPE, there would be no educational works set in any other way.

The Keyboard

THE MONOTYPE is one of those modern marvels of machinery that performs operations formerly considered impossible to achieve by anything save the human hand. The MONOTYPE makes type—and not only makes it, but sets it; sets it every whit as well as the best compositor could, and from six to ten times faster.

It makes new type for every job. Therefore, there is no such thing in MONOTYPE work as worn letters or muddy printing. Every letter and character stands out clear and sharp.

A High Sign of Quality

Corrections are very easily made—much more easily than in any other form of machine composition. Accent marks, algebraic and geometrical symbols, foreign alphabets and all the unusual characters that educational work needs are at the command of the MONOTYPE owner.

Best of all, MONOTYPE work, with all its high quality, is economical.

The next time you send a job to a printer, *specify* MONOTYPE composition. If you want to see an example of it, see the new *Encylopædia Britannica* or the pages of practically any high-class magazine printed in the United States.

MONOTYPE composition can be had in Philadelphia on any jobs, large or small, by applying to

The Caster

THE JOHN C. WINSTON CO.
Printers
1006-1016 Arch Street

THE GREAT WAR

A Series of Non-Partisan Volumes on the Causes Of and Motives For; on the Mobilization of the Moral and Physical Forces; on the Conduct of the Hostilities; and on the Final Results.

ELABORATELY ILLUSTRATED

BY TRAINED HISTORIANS AND MILITARY AND NAVAL EXPERTS

GEORGE H. ALLEN, Ph.D., CAPTAIN WHITEHEAD, U. S. A., ADMIRAL CHADWICK, U. S. N.

AND INTRODUCTION BY

Hon. WILLIAM HOWARD TAFT

Absolutely impartial—"Sure to attract attention from discriminating readers."—*Providence Journal.*

The President and the Chief Justice, the New York and other Libraries, Messrs. J. P. Morgan & Co., Mr. James J. Hill, and thousands of other prominent men and institutions have this book on their shelves. And with very good reason, for the interest in the subject is intense.

Ex-President TAFT in his introduction to this series tells us that when a cataclysm like the present war in Europe makes a turning point in human progress we are led to study the causes.

Are you, as are so many others, wondering what has caused this momentous conflict that has so convulsed the whole current of human life and thought?

Would you like to know what motives and causes brought about the catastrophe; what spiritual or moral considerations drove the nations to the point of going to war; how they mobilized their military, naval, financial, and other forces; exactly how hostilities progressed; and the economic and political results?

The immediate success of this series of *inexpensive* volumes by trained historians and military and naval experts proves that many thoughtful persons, and institutions of many kinds, are glad to have such volumes devoted to these subjects for reading and reference *now.*

The New York *Evening Post*, calls it "a real addition to the literature of this great disaster, "and adds that "it would be difficult to name another volume that attempts to do just what this one does and does it so well."

The *New York Tribune* considers the series "likely to become the most serious and serviceable popular-scholarly history of the war in all its phases that we shall have."

The *New York Times* commends it for "its elaborate illustrations and its unusually non-partisan spirit."

The *Sun*, New York, feels the same way about it and calls it "a handsome specimen of typography."

The first volume, *complete in itself*, is devoted to a consideration of the motives and causes which brought about the war. Would you like to have it, with details of special offer to *advance* subscribers, sent to you so that you can look it over at your leisure?

Will you send us first payment of one dollar or return the volume, *uncut,* within three days?

Use this convenient little coupon. Just pin to your letter-head. To GEORGE BARRIE'S SONS, 1313 Walnut St., Philadelphia Established 1873. GRAND PRIX and 18 medals and diplomas

Yes

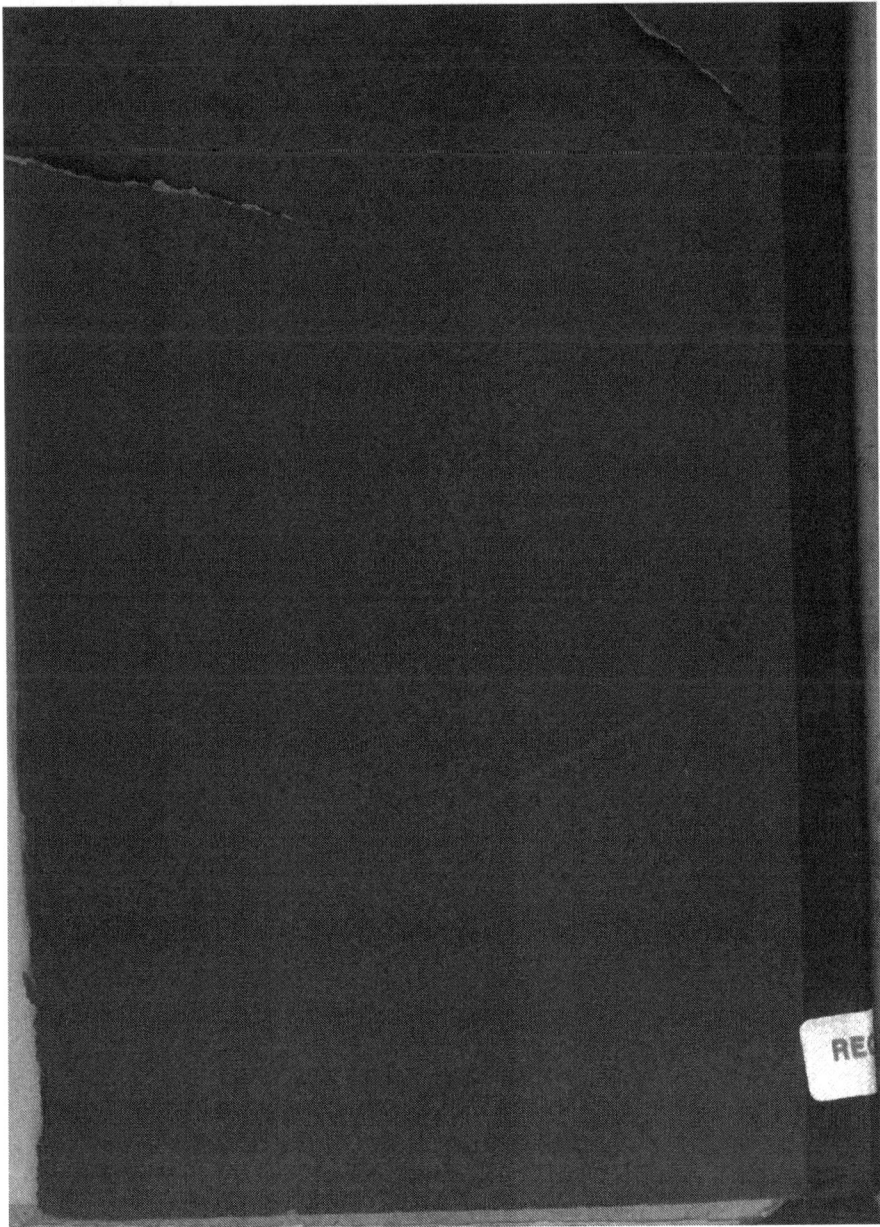

Lightning Source UK Ltd.
Milton Keynes UK
UKHW021218271220
375792UK00005B/1228

9 781377 157931